LUCRATIVE EXITS

The No BS Insider's Guide to Selling Your Business for Its Highest Value Today or Tomorrow

Gregg Kunz, CBI, M&AMI

This book is dedicated to my father, John, from whom I learned most about leadership, independence, calling foul within the corporate world, and having an unrelenting confidence to get back up whenever knocked down. He also instilled the importance of having the moral and emotional courage to challenge the status quo to do what is fair and right - as painful as it can be, but which has its own reward and satisfaction.

CONTENTS

market but from within your circle. Unwilling partners or family members can pose significant obstacles to a smooth sale. Multiple stakeholders mean multiple emotions, and this can complicate matters.

Transparency is the solution. As a business broker, I meet with all stakeholders, explaining the process and addressing concerns to help find common ground. And sometimes, bringing in third parties, like financial advisors or exit planners, can offer clarity, help align interests, and get all stakeholders on the same page.

YOUR QUESTIONS ANSWERED

Throughout my years of practice, I've been asked countless questions. If you are considering selling your business, you probably wonder:

- *"How much is my business worth?"*
- *"How long will the sale process take?"*
- *"What are the tax implications of the sale?"*
- *"How do we ensure confidentiality during the sale process?"*
- *"How can I get the highest sale price?"*

Some questions aren't for me to answer, like gauging if the sale proceeds will support your lifestyle. However, a competent broker should confidently address common concerns after an in-depth, honest, and objective discussion of your goals. Business brokers are at heart also problem solvers. They do not have all of the answers but good ones should be able to call on their trusted network to provide you with the professional expertise who can answer your questions and temper your fears.

Many business owners approach the sale with a degree of suspicion, especially toward brokers. It's a fear I've encountered often: "Will the broker truly prioritize my interests?"

While some newer brokers might focus on quick sales to cover their bills, seasoned brokers know the value of building relationships, adhering to process, and keeping the client's timeframe first and foremost. Properly pricing a business and ensuring a smooth transition takes precedence over rushed, poorly conceived transactions.

My journey from the corporate world, being at senior levels where every detail mattered, has instilled in me the importance of preparation. I've been a business owner three times over, and I've tasted both the bitterness of getting less than I should have and the sweetness of a high-value exit. This first-hand experience allows me to understand the nuances and challenges of the sale process, ensuring a smooth transition for my clients.

Since I handle the intricacies of selling, my clients can be 100% focused on their business operations during the process. Some owners will take their foot off the gas, thinking, "Oh, now that I'm selling, I don't have to work as hard." That's the death knell right there.

I believe in thoroughness. My documents provide comprehensive information about the business. These aren't just a reflection of the business; they're a reflection of the broker. A half-hearted job gives a poor impression of both.

Our results speak for themselves. We sell better than 90% of the businesses we bring to market. Is it because we're magicians? No. We focus solely on great businesses, not perfect businesses, and not businesses without blemishes. But we understand the imperfections. Any of these can become objections or obstacles in the sale process. We identify them and formulate solutions early in the sale process so they don't become deal stoppers. Identifying and addressing potential roadblocks ensures that when speaking with a prospective buyer that the broker and seller are perceived as credible business people, not salespeople.

My clients appreciate that I don't sugarcoat the facts. I strive to tell business owners what they need to hear rather than what they want to hear. Is it painful at times? Absolutely. But if your broker leads you to believe that everything about your business is great, it's probably time to consider interviewing another broker.

In the following chapters, I'll share strategies and insights into business selling, covering topics such as:

- Sale preparation
- Building an advisory team
- Valuation
- Finding the right buyer
- Marketing strategies
- Negotiation tips
- Financing
- Closing the deal

I'll also include plenty of anecdotes and tips that I have learned along the way.

LIFE BEYOND YOUR BUSINESS

Most business owners embarked on their entrepreneurial journey with a vision. That vision becomes their destination. Over time, they find that their reasons for diving into the business world have been realized, and a new chapter awaits them.

Whether it's retiring with dreams of traveling, spending time with family, or even pursuing an entirely different direction, like returning to school, the financial freedom from a successful business exit provides the runway to make those dreams a reality. Despite making a great income, I once had a client who desired to completely disengage from his business to indulge in his dream of playing golf every day without any distractions - including even minor and infrequent calls from the office. His dream was to be entirely out, and he trusted our firm to make his dream a reality. Success is relative to you and you alone, as are your goals and dreams. Everyone's interpretation of success varies.

One clear distinction I've observed is between those running *from* their businesses and those running *towards* a life they've dreamed of. The latter usually realize significantly more value from their exit and their dream becomes their reality.

Having been in the business owner's shoes, I've painfully experienced the lack of guidance when I made my decision to sell . I ventured into this book to bridge that gap for others. The transition from business to the "feet in the sand, drink in hand" dream isn't as straightforward as many perceive.

By following the steps in this book, you will have a more rewarding exit, and your business will thrive in the interim. You'll enjoy better sleep, longer or more frequent vacations, and more free time. Ultimately, instead of being consumed by your business, you'll control it. Ready to make that shift? There's plenty to do; let's get started.

- Gregg Kunz

CHAPTER ONE
Motivations & Market Dynamics

Selling a business isn't just a decision—it's a journey. It's a process. And throughout our time together in this book, you'll hear a lot about that word: process. Because, believe me, process drives results. And an excellently executed process? That will drive excellent results.

One of the important aspects here is learning to expect and anticipate the unexpected. Unanticipated issues and questions will arise at the most inopportune time, and that's a guarantee. But if you're well-prepared and follow the process, you'll navigate those challenges efficiently and effectively.

I've seen something all too often: a business owner wakes up one day, looks around, and thinks, "Today's the day I sell my business." But making such a spur-of-the-moment decision isn't the key to a desirable outcome. It simply doesn't work that way. The sale of your business doesn't (and shouldn't) begin on the day you decide to put it on the market for sale. A successful exit requires time, preparation, and ideally should begin as far in advance as possible.

The selling process can seem either too simple or overwhelmingly complex to many business owners. Some see it as an easy task,

1

while others consider it a towering mountain they must conquer—all while keeping their business running. But here's the thing: it isn't either of those extremes.

Yes, it's not a straightforward process. But with the proper guidance and approach, it's also not insurmountable. The trick? Taking it in bite-sized pieces and breaking things down to address one by one. And that's where experts like business brokers come into play. Having a seasoned guide by your side, someone who's been there and done that will make all the difference. Your business broker is not just an advisor but a leader who'll lead you through every step of the way, ensuring a less stressful and ultimately more successful outcome.

DECODING THE DECISION TO SELL

Every business owner's journey is unique, but several shared reasons might lead an owner to consider selling their venture.

- **Retirement Plans:** Whether it's an early exit or a delayed one, retirement is often the driving force behind selling.
- **Health Challenges:** Illness or other health problems can push an owner towards selling their life's work.
- **Business Performance:** Some owners face obstacles they feel ill-equipped to overcome.
- **Partnership Conflicts:** Disagreements with business partners can compel an owner to step away.
- **Burnout:** The relentless pace and pressures of business can wear out even the most passionate owner.
- **Growth Barriers:** Another decisive factor is feeling stagnant and unable to push the business beyond certain boundaries.

- **Customers & Employees:** Neither of these groups are always a joy to work with and it's not uncommon for an owner to wonder why their efforts to please or care for others leave them unfulfilled and unhappy.

But there's a flip side too. Some owners view their current enterprise as a stepping stone to something larger. With all the valuable lessons they've gleaned, they're eager to leap into a new business venture, armed with enhanced knowledge and fewer blind spots. Their aim? To be more strategic, efficient, and ultimately successful in their next endeavor. Remember, hindsight is 20/20, but what you do with those insights is what ultimately counts.

The Misconceptions Surrounding Business Sales

There's one fairy-tale notion that many business owners hold dear: "If someone came and offered me a great price, I would sell." Here's the reality check: unless you're actively looking to sell, the chances of someone arriving with a sack full of cash for your enterprise are slim to none.

And then there are those unsolicited promises from third parties, most of which are less than genuine. They'll claim to have a buyer ready and waiting for your business. A word to the wise: such promises often fall flat. If a broker or anyone else tells you they have a buyer, they'd better have one. This is why you need to work with someone you can trust and someone who has a depth of experience in selling businesses. As you contemplate the sale of your business, prioritize getting to know brokers in your market. An initial conversation can reveal much about their character, approach, and honesty. Remember, you're not just entering a transaction with them; you're embarking on a relationship from the onset of the sale process to the closing table - and likely to be a relationship spanning many months.

The Surprising Reasons Businesses Go Up for Sale

You might be nodding your head, thinking, "That's all fine and good for everyone else but I'm ready to sell my business now." But here's something many overlook: *while you may be ready, is your business?* This is a point many business owners haven't pondered and I often get blank stares in return when I bring up this subject. However, you, the owner, and the business must be poised and absolutely ready to sell.

Let's face it: Business owners, like everyone else, have spoken and unspoken reasons and motivations for selling. Often, the reason they provide for selling isn't always the whole truth. It's not about deception; it's human nature. They might not want to admit, even to themselves, that they've grown weary of dealing with demanding customers or that some days, their employees feel more like a painful burden than an asset. The reason for selling your business is deeply personal and unique to you.

A Serious Golf Addiction

To illustrate my point, let me share a story. I once worked with the owners of a wildly successful business. They each worked a mere 20 hours every other week and each took home over $300,000 annually. They were living what many would call the entrepreneurial dream. And yet, when I asked them why they were selling such a thriving enterprise, their answer was simple: they had enough saved up and wanted no interruptions in their early retirement. One owner humorously mentioned wanting to develop a "serious golf addiction." He laughed when he said it but it was clear that he was absolutely serious about his personal motivation to sell.

While a buyer might be looking in from the outside, wondering why someone would give up such a lucrative existence, remember that everyone has their own definition of success and fulfillment. Some find joy in their day-to-day business engagements, while others, after years of dedication, want to pursue other passions and interests. Selling is about you. Your motivations to sell are yours alone. Embrace them.

BALANCING PERSONAL AND FINANCIAL FACTORS IN SELLING YOUR BUSINESS

The balance between personal and financial reasons for selling is delicate. Business owners often grapple with the uncertainty of when to pull the trigger and place their business on the market. What's more pressing? Your health and personal life or the financial factors that surround your business?

Unfortunately, personal reasons, such as health and family matters, can make the sale of a business a pressing necessity. Think of preparing to sell as setting up a Will or Estate Plan for your business. Just as it's a mistake to pass away without a Will, and leaving your estate's distribution to the whims of the state, not preparing your business for a potential sale is a significant misstep and, in the worst cases, a devastating blow to your family's financial well-being and future security.

If unexpected events arise – and they often do – your preparation ensures you're not caught off guard. It means you have set your business up to be desirable to potential buyers even under unforeseen circumstances. As brokers, we are limited to the hand we're dealt. However, any bit of planning and preparation can tip the scales in the seller's favor for a successful exit no matter the circumstances. In addition to preparing your business for an unexpected sale it just makes plain sense to know the value of your business. That is, what is the price that the business is likely to sell for.

Before diving into the financial or economic factors, let me highlight a tool in our arsenal: the Broker's Opinion of Value. While it might sound a lot like valuation, they are distinct from one another. Only certified valuation professionals can issue a "valuation." In our realm, as brokers, we're determining the most probable selling price range for a third-party buyer, not for the purposes of a Buy-Sell agreement or a Divorce, where 'value' may take on an entirely different meaning. Business brokers are completing transactions in the market each and every day. The combination of the analytical tools they use, their business acumen, and their experience in the business sale marketplace will provide you with the most factual understanding of the value drivers in a sale and the most likely selling price range.

Our goal isn't to forecast every potential scenario but to evaluate how the business would fare in a realistic market scenario. Economic fluctuations, market saturation, regulatory shifts, declining profits, or even your product becoming obsolete (think of VHS tapes and tape cassettes) can have pronounced impacts on a business's appeal. But as brokers, our North Star is the most probable selling price range to a third-party buyer.

Contrary to personal reasons that demand swift decisions, economic factors usually offer a much longer runway in determining if this may be the time to sell. Well-run businesses with diverse income streams and delivering consistent profits can often navigate economic challenges unless they face the sunset of their product or service. If your gut feeling foretells a declining market or an unfavorable economic trend, it's a cue to ready your business for sale. And remember, the *average* time to sell a business ranges from five and ten months. Depending on the business you are in, the readiness of the business for sale, and changing market conditions, a sale may take a year or longer.

Changing Market Conditions in Business Sales

As business owners, it's easy to get lost in the noise of daily headlines. We read about the economy's trajectory, unemployment trends, and more. These, however, are macro conditions. For the Main Street and Premier Main Street business, like the automotive repair shop serving its community for decades, these broader economic waves might have a less direct impact than you'd think. So, if the general economy is going south, it doesn't mean your business is on the same path. Strong, well-operated, and well-prepared businesses tend to sell for premium and realistic prices regardless of the macroeconomic environment. In the past couple of years interest rates began climbing quickly. Both buyers and sellers called with similar comments with the same underlying concern; "This must be a bad time to sell/buy a business." Let me assure you, *great businesses are always in demand.*

One of the potential pitfalls is being overly reactive to these national or global market indicators. Buyers and sellers alike can fall into this trap, assuming that high interest rates make it a bad time to buy or sell. Remember, a great business paired with a knowledgeable and confident broker can create a transaction structure to mitigate external circumstances beyond the business owner's or buyer's control. Focus on your geographic and industry market. Understand the nuances, and if you're a business whose customers come from a close geographic radius, the local market conditions genuinely matter more than national market conditions. Larger global enterprises will need to take a broader view, but the principle remains: know your market intimately.

In fast-evolving market trends, it's common for both buyers and sellers to become confused and forget reality. I once worked with a client who owned a multi-location driving school. We met with two prospective buyers, partners who were very well-qualified in every way. They stated that the business met nearly all their criteria. However, in the end, they backed out, citing concerns about the future impact of self-driving cars on the driving school industry. Their reasoning was rather amusing. It seemed to be more of a convenient excuse rather than a concern grounded in fact. It was their absolute barrier to moving forward despite the fact that every other financial and operational aspect of the business met their criteria. Think about it, even if self-driving cars become the norm, there will still be a need for driver's education and licensing. Even in an automated world, people must understand how to operate vehicles. What may happen many decades into the future should not stand in the way of buying a business today, and evolving the business as industry trends may necessitate. Don't let distant, speculative concerns overshadow the value of a business, nor allow buyers with false objections to get in the way of the truth.

IMPACTS OF THE DIGITAL AGE

Entering the business brokerage world in the digital age has been a blessing. The ease with which businesses can now be presented and marketed is remarkable. We have more tools at our disposal than in the past, from specialized platforms to targeted social media campaigns. Gone are the days when placing a classified ad in a newspaper was our primary avenue. At the same time, do not conclude that selling a business in the Digital Age is easy. It may help to locate a buyer, but as you will learn, not all self-titled buyers are real buyers and the real work for the broker actually begins after a serious buyer is engaged.

The digital age has streamlined processes across the board. It has created efficiencies across all industries but it's also brought challenges to others, particularly the ever-present shadow of e-commerce. Every package dropped off at a doorstep is a testament to evolving business models impacting one another, sometimes to the point of extinction.

Whether a local bookstore or a pet store, businesses, especially retailers, feel the pinch from e-commerce giants. The message here is clear: innovation waits for no one. Think of the once-popular products and services that are now relics of the past, whether buggy whips, VHS tapes, or taxis. If you don't keep an ear to the ground and understand the changing preferences and technological advancements, you might find yourself blindsided when you decide it's time to sell.

As you contemplate the sale or purchase of a business, remember to strike a balance. Understand the macro, but act on the micro. Embrace the digital, but don't forget the timeless principles of business. And always, always stay informed and remain adaptable.

WALKING A MILE IN THE BUYER'S SHOES

When you're on the cusp of selling your business, understanding the mindset of potential buyers will make all the difference. While business owners like yourself may be natural risk-takers, buyers, especially first-timers, are often treading in unfamiliar waters. Their initial enthusiasm can be overshadowed by anxiety about potential risks, especially as they come to grips with the weight of their impending purchase. Unlike being an employee, where there's a safety net in the form of consistent paychecks and set responsibilities, owning a business means shouldering every responsibility, rain or shine. There is no need to over-emphasize this to a prospective buyer, but providing encouragement will go a long way to selling your business. This encouragement will ideally come from you rather than only the broker whose words of encouragement may be received as a sales tactic. Let's face the reality that the vast majority of the population believe that brokers, be they auto, insurance, or business brokers are trying to sell them something. Selling a business must be a collaborative process with the business owner and the broker.

One effective strategy I've always believed in is proactive problem-solving. Anticipate the buyer's concerns and be prepared with answers. Full disclosure of issues, potential or other, need to be shared with your broker. This will enable you both to have an articulate and believable answer when a buyer asks rather than being blindsided.

A few years back, I worked with a very successful and especially profitable hail restoration business focused on the automotive sector (paintless dent removal). It was easy to anticipate a very real concern for a buyer and one that, if we could not overcome, would kill the prospects for a sale – hail is a weather-dependent event. It is an unpredictable act of nature. It would be folly for the broker or seller to try to convince a buyer otherwise, and I knew that it was likely the first and most insurmountable objection from a buyer unfamiliar with the industry. Remember that the vast majority of buyers have little understanding of your industry. You are the expert in your industry and you should not allow their incorrect assumptions to remain.

I spent days researching all I could about Colorado's weather and, specifically, the frequency of significant hail events. In conjunction with Colorado State University and NOAA, I gained access to detailed weather records spanning the last 140 years (and plenty were of the handwritten type). What we were able to document was that in the prior 140 years, there was only one year in which there was not a significant hail event across the business's geographic service area. Because these events created a backlog of work for as much as 36 months, the actual risk to the business was small. The *perceived* risk was large, but the *actual* risk was minimal.

If a business owner dismisses a buyer's fear (risk) or attempts to hide or gloss over a perceived risk, it will kill a deal. Smart brokers (and I consider myself one) dig deeply to determine real and potential areas of risk and to address them early in the process. If you identify, surface, and address a risk with a buyer early in the conversation, it will likely fall by the wayside and not derail an otherwise good transaction. Never underestimate the impact of perceived risk from the buyer's perspective, as it may kill the transaction even at the closing table. Remember that by surfacing and addressing perceived risks you will build credibility with the buyer which can make the purchase of your business even more compelling.

A Final Note About Transparency and Preparation

Transparency is the foundation of any trustworthy business transaction. As a business owner, it's not uncommon to have specific details about your business you might want to keep hidden. These could be minor oversights or more significant issues that feel embarrassing or, quite frankly, detrimental to a successful sale.

Conversations with buyers, especially the savvy ones we aim to attract, are a series of questions and answers. They will probe and ask predictable questions, as well as some you'd never anticipate. In these exchanges, any weaknesses, obstacles, or potential deal breakers in your business will come to light— if not early in the conversation then most likely during due diligence. If these aren't disclosed and addressed upfront, you can be sure the lender or the buyer's advisors will catch them, potentially jeopardizing the entire sale.

This is not to say that you should surface a risk that is part and parcel of any business. For example, attracting and retaining staff. Staffing is *always* a challenge for every business. Is it a risk that needs to be surfaced if the buyer asks what other risks they should be aware of? I am of the opinion that this one in particular, while a risk, is so prevalent across all businesses that it need not be surfaced. Is it a risk or simply a normal part of business? This does not mean to duck the question if asked, but to answer it appropriately. The correct way to answer the question is, "As with all businesses, attracting and retaining employees is important, and a smart owner should always be looking for talent as well as treating their employees well, as we do".

If, as a broker, I'm unaware of both perceived and actual risk-related questions, and how the owner will address them, the ramifications can be catastrophic. Deals can collapse, and in some instances, the business might even become unsaleable. It's a heavy price to pay when months spent in the sales preparation and process lead to a dead end. This becomes a severe time waste and can compromise the deal structure and leave significant value on the table. Never let your broker be surprised because you failed to make them aware of a potential area of risk, and if it is an adverse material fact, you *must* disclose it. Trust me, honesty counts.

A TESTAMENT TO PROPER PREPARATION

I recall a business owner reaching out shortly after 2022 wrapped up, eager to sell. Our initial meeting made it apparent that they were perhaps the most properly and well-prepared seller client I'd had the pleasure of working with. Their financials were up-to-date, tax returns filed, and they meticulously documented everything spanning the last three to five years.

But more than just being organized, they understood their business inside and out—from knowing their numbers to having every process and procedure fully documented. They were significantly more well-prepared than most, and we valued their business by over $600,000 more than the other broker they had spoken to. The overall quality of their business supported a market multiple at the highest end of the range, and we were absolutely prepared to defend our value determination to a buyer, a lender, and the lender's valuation expert. If I could point to why this was one of our most successful outcomes it would be this: the owner took the preparation process to heart more than a year before he contacted me. He was ready and his business was ready. It paid off in spades.

KEY TAKEAWAYS

⊃ Selling a business is not a spontaneous decision but a well-planned process. A well-executed process drives successful outcomes.

- Market conditions evolve and change over time. If your business is not evolving to meet these changes, the value of your business today may be far different than when it is your time to sell.

- Don't get lost in macroeconomic conditions; focus on your specific market. Understand its nuances and adapt to changes while considering the timeless principles of business.

- Preparation results in a successful sale. It's not just about the day you decide to sell; it's about getting your business ready for the sale from the time you open your doors.

- The sale process is a collaboration with your broker. They are experts in the process - you are the expert in your business. Don't disrupt their process and don't have them try to become the expert on your business. In short, know each other's role.

- Viewing your business through the eyes of a buyer is critical to a successful exit and identifying perceived and actual risks, and how to address questions for each is imperative.

- Preparing to sell is not a one-time event, nor is it a ton of work. It is process-driven and the process must be allowed to unfold.

CHAPTER TWO
WHEN PREPARATION MEETS OPPORTUNITY

J
ust like you invested time, energy, and passion into building your venture, you want to ensure you exit at the right time and for the right price. We've all heard the saying, "Failing to prepare is preparing to fail." This couldn't be more accurate when it comes to selling your business.

Consider this: If you're selling a product, you'd think about its presentation, right? Packaging, marketing, and positioning all play a role. Your business isn't any different. Preparing to sell is about looking at your company not just through your eyes but through the eyes of potential buyers. It's easy to say, "My business is fantastic; who wouldn't want it?" You might be familiar with "The Golden Rule" of treating others how you'd want to be treated. But when selling a business, I'd urge you to follow "The Platinum Rule:" Treat potential buyers how they want to be treated. That is, view your business through their eyes. This shift in perspective can make a world of difference.

By focusing on the right aspects of your business, you can fetch the highest exit price, and your business will be genuinely appealing to potential buyers. And trust me, if you diligently follow the steps we'll discuss, you might even nail down a price higher than your initial listing price. How? You'll attract multiple offers by making your business irresistible, fueling a competitive buying environment.

Emotions as the Invisible Players in Your Sale

How do you determine if you're emotionally and practically prepared to sell your business? The answer is more complex than you might expect.

The sale of a business isn't just a financial transaction; it's an emotional one, too. Many owners underestimate the intensity of emotions that arise during the sale process. In all cases, it's vital to recognize that selling a business will feel more like a stressful marathon than a sprint to a celebratory finish line. Keep your eye on the goal and your emotions under wrap.

My experience shows that you've conquered half the battle if you can set your emotions aside and trust a seasoned expert to guide you. But remember, it's easier said than done. Every business sale has its obstacles, and it's a roller coaster of emotions. But by leaving those feelings at the door and letting an expert guide you, the process can be educational and profitable.

Practical Preparedness

On the practical side, brace yourself for some news: your business might not be in its prime selling condition. A successful sale demands thorough preparation to make every aspect of your business as presentable and appealing as possible to potential buyers.

Consider franchises, for example. They're desirable because they come with an established playbook. Everything is set - from hiring procedures to dispute resolutions. Buyers prefer businesses that don't require them to reinvent the wheel. If you're prepared with a plan for the buyer, you're setting your business up for a seamless transition. And remember, your definition of "simple and easy" might not be the same as a buyer's. This difference in perspective is natural, but having a comprehensive plan will help bridge that gap.

LOOPING IN YOUR SPOUSE

And oh, a little side note, but it's a biggie: Have you spoken to your spouse about selling? If they're not on board or unprepared for the post-sale changes in your lifestyle, you could be in for a bumpy ride. Get them in the loop to make sure that they are onboard with your plan.

REALITY CHECK

When considering a sale, it's not always only about the highest price but may also be about legacy in the community and the welfare of employees. During our initial interactions, one of the primary questions I ask owners involves aspirations - not just about the sale, but life post-sale. Do they care what type of personality the buyer has? After all, once you ride off into the sunset is it especially important who owns the business? Perceptions may be far different than the reality and the facts need to be understood before your decision to sell is put into action. It's essential because there's a sea of misleading information out there. Many owners are shocked when faced with unexpected realities like:

- The sale price might not match their expectations.
- The after-tax proceeds will be significantly less than the sale price.
- Employees might be treated differently under a new owner.
- The new owner's personality or moral compass may be different from yours.
- The business's legacy could fade in the eyes of customers and the market you have served over many years.

If price is your sole focus, you might compromise on the buyer's nature. But if legacy matters more, you could trade a bit of the price for the right buyer. Change to your business post-sale is inevitable. Accepting this can save you from lingering regrets. In your early conversations with brokers you need to share your motivations, concerns, and what you envision the most appropriate buyer to look like. Whether they are like you or not does not mean the business will not thrive under their leadership. Be clear when stating your motivations for the sale to your broker. This will not only begin to build a strong working relationship but it will enable them to begin to understand the type of buyer which will be a good match with you as well as the business.

It's not just the buyer who will be scrutinizing your business. Banks, appraisers, attorneys, accountants, and the occasional un-solicited advice-giver are all weighing in. And while we might all appreciate a bit of flattery now and then, this isn't the time for it. It's the time for clear-eyed assessments. Every business has flaws, but with a little effort, there's always room for improvement - and making time for that improvement will pay off at the closing table. Don't feel overwhelmed by the changes or improvements the broker may suggest. They tend to be much less costly and time-consuming than you might expect. Great brokers know what savvy buyers are looking for, and failing to make these small recommended improvements will cost you at the closing table.

Your perceptions might not align with the market reality. While you might see untapped potential everywhere, a savvy buyer will wonder, "If these are such golden opportunities, why haven't they been pursued?" You must be prepared to answer this question as it is certain to arise. If you do not have a sensible and believable answer, the buyer will not buy into it. Falling on your sword, allowing yourself to show you are as vulnerable as others, and truth-telling tend to be well-received by buyers and may help to strengthen the buyer-seller relationship early in the process.

Rely on the broker's experience and expertise when determining your business's worth. And no, that doesn't mean turning to friends, spouses, accountants, or even your gut feeling. Trust someone who sells businesses day in and day out. Brokers are serious about the determination of the value of your business. They undergo rigorous education to understand how to value a business, and they are the ones who have to defend that value determination to buyers, lenders, and the lenders' business appraisers. They've seen the patterns, the pitfalls, and the triumphs. As for your business's potential? While it's important information, it's generally not what determines the final price. In today's world, the price is a function of the overall financial benefit to the owner. Period.

THE HUMBLE ROAD TO SUCCESS

I continue to be amazed by the success stories that come from what society often dubs as "blue-collar" businesses. These hard-working men and women, covered in the grit and grime of a day's labor, do not fit the stereotypical image of success. Yet, behind the facade, they have stories of tenacity, humility, wisdom and the wealth that would put many white-collar achievements to shame.

Pat was a prime example. He hailed from a lineage of auto mechanics—those dedicated individuals with perpetually darkened hands who work diligently on what we choose not to. Society rarely gives them much in the way of recognition as we tend to do with 'white collars'. Pat found his calling in auto body repair, where he channeled his passion for perfection, pleasing others, and his artistic touch.

His reputation became legendary across Denver and its neighboring states. People would travel for hours to get their cars worked on by him. But as with most success stories, there were times when he had to make challenging decisions grounded only by the facts he had collected and his gut feeling.

In many ways, the conventional auto body business model is dictated by insurance companies. These giants set the terms, sometimes compromising the quality of repair in favor of speed and cost-efficiency. Pat, however, valued the artistry of his work above all else. He boldly decided to cut ties with the insurance companies who sent him business but also dictated all aspects of the repair. It seemed to Pat that he was sacrificing the security of guaranteed work for the integrity of his craftsmanship and that eventually drove him to cut ties.

The result? An 80% drop in business from the insurance companies that had kept him busy year after year. But instead of panicking or returning to the hands that had fed him, Pat turned adversity into opportunity. He invested in an industry consultant, who, even though two time zones away, provided invaluable guidance and insight. With a roadmap tailored uniquely for him and a newfound advisory team, including a savvy CPA, Pat turned his business around, doubled revenues, tripled his profits, and expanded his operations.

When I met Pat, he was not only ready to sell but had established an extensive plan that made his business an attractive proposition for potential buyers. The net after-tax proceeds from the sale promised him a comfortable retirement and a legacy for his family. Not only that, but the changes and improvements he made to the business allowed him to bank plenty of cash in the years preceding the sale.

This isn't just Pat's story. It's the story of countless business owners who have found their path to greatness despite challenges, humble beginnings, or lack of formal education. It's about recognizing one's strengths and, more importantly, one's weaknesses. It's about seeking help when needed, continuous learning, and, above all, keeping the integrity of the work at the forefront.

Pat's journey from a dedicated artisan to a thriving business owner wasn't without its challenges. But with a trusted advisory team, including experts like consultants and CPAs, he charted his path to success. It's a lesson for every business owner: you don't have to know it all. Surrounding yourself with the right team can take you from where you are to where you want to be. *Being humble enough to ask for help is not a weakness but a strength.*

Financial Health: The Heartbeat of Your Sale

The financial health of your business is pivotal. A business with declining financial performance is especially hard to sell. If you're wondering who'd be interested in a business that's not thriving, you're not alone. In the corporate realm, there's often a safety net, a salary, and incentives for turnarounds. But in the business owner's world, the financial risks are yours alone. Every decision impacts your pocket directly. Trust me, there are extremely few buyers willing to acquire a failing business and, as importantly, virtually zero lenders who will participate in the deal. In the unlikely event that you can find a willing buyer, be prepared for little in the way of a cash down payment as well as financing the sale with Seller Financing with future payments contingent on the buyer's ability to turn the business around. Buyers will want to be cautious with the cash they have for a down payment in case the business continues to fail.

Don't misunderstand me; growth isn't the sole indicator of a business's success. Once they've achieved a comfortable plateau, many owners rightly choose to enjoy the fruits of their labor. Such businesses can be delightful to sell. However, selling becomes a complex challenge when the decline is due to the failure of the owner to adjust to industry changes or poor management. If you find yourself in this tricky position, your broker must have the ability to craft a compelling and credible narrative that resonates with potential buyers.

Turning around financial health isn't about slashing prices or reducing salaries. Instead, consider consulting with a proficient fractional CFO or CEO. Explore the root causes of your financial challenges and get referrals to experts who can help. I've observed a recurring theme: Businesses often falter when they skimp on marketing, advertising, or customer relations. Think of advertising as an investment, similar to building your retirement fund. Marketing and advertising can be the quickest path to increasing financial performance.

Some may believe that cutting costs will increase the financial performance of the business. In the very near term this may be likely, but cutting the wrong costs can cripple a business for the long term. *Saving your way to success rarely works.*

If you want a litmus test for your financial records, get them under the lens of a business broker and at least two SBA bankers. These folks will let you know if your financial performance and documentation are up to the mark. Your lender, being the most risk-averse of all parties to a transaction, will be the judge of your accounting and financial reporting, so getting their nod is imperative.

And if there's an issue? Rely on your broker to connect you to qualified and experienced bookkeepers and accountants to rectify any problems. However, remember that if you've been sloppy or dishonest, there may be little that can be done.

Financial or accounting missteps can come in various forms. You must be cautious, whether it's inconsistencies between tax returns and income statements or dubious handling of personal expenses through the business. Always maintain detailed documentation, especially for any personal expenses that you hope can be added back to increase the business's value.

Lastly, you're accountable for your tax return, not your tax preparer. Get someone you trust who offers more than just tax preparation – someone who provides advice and guidance.

I've had my trusted tax expert for over three decades, and he's been my sounding board for not just tax matters but business, family, and estate decisions. Such relationships are invaluable.

The clarity of your financial statements is as important as the numbers themselves. While you're juggling roles as a business owner, prioritizing bookkeeping might seem less urgent. However, a solid financial foundation can streamline your business operations and make it more attractive to buyers or render it unsalable.

What Buyers Really Want

Many people, buyers and sellers alike, get caught up in the allure of top-line revenues. But is that what truly matters? No, in fact, revenue has little to zero impact on the value (price) of a business. Profitability, on the other hand, lies mainly within an owner's control. Savvy owners know the ins and outs of their expenses and how to maximize their bottom line. At the end of the day, the value of, and the price paid for a business is based on the financial benefit realized by an owner in terms of profit, not revenue. In the business brokerage world this financial benefit is called *Seller Discretionary Earnings* (SDE). The terms *Owner Benefit* and *Adjusted Cash Flow* may also be used but I caution using adjusted cash flow as it can have various applications when speaking about the financials of a business. For this reason I will use the term Seller Discretionary Earnings, or SDE, as we move forward. There is another term which you may have heard of: *EBITDA* or *Adjusted EBITDA*. How do they differ? EBITDA, as expanded on later in this book is an acronym for Earnings Before Interest, Taxes, Depreciation, and Amortization. It is used primarily for evaluating and determining the value (sale price) of businesses which approach and exceed $1,000,000 in SDE (comparatively speaking). As we move further upmarket above the Main Street business sale marketplace we may also use Adjusted EBITDA. This essentially uses the same (larger) add backs but not the wages paid to the owner, as well as their associated company-paid payroll taxes. For the vast majority of Main and Premier Main Street businesses SDE is used with the assumption that the buyer will be an owner-operator of the business. Private Equity, Synergistic, and Strategic buyers are normally ones where there will not be an owner-operator, but a general manager or equivalent.

So, if revenue and net profit are not the basis for determining the sales price range and SDE is, what exactly is the definition of SDE? SDE refers to the true financial benefit of a single owner of a business - above and beyond the net income shown on the Profit and Loss statement (P&L) or tax return. To calculate SDE we begin with the net income (or net loss) and add back the following expenses which appear on the P&L: owner's salary, payroll taxes paid by the company on the owner's salary, amortization, interest paid, depreciation, non-recurring expenses, discretionary expenses, and *select and fully documented* personal expenses of the owner paid by the business. Personal expenses like Health and Life Insurance, IRA contributions, and company-paid matches to IRA contributions are customarily added back and acceptable by a lender in determining SDE with accompanying documentation. Cell phone services, travel, meals, and the owner's vehicle expenses may be accepted by a buyer in determining SDE but lenders usually remove these in their internal credit decision making. That trip to Costa Rica or the golf club membership may or may not be acceptable to the lender. Always maintain complete documentation for any and every expense that is indeed a personal expense but do not be surprised if the lender tosses them aside.

There are other expenses which may need to be adjusted for in calculating SDE. One that we see quite frequently is the wages associated with family members who have a full, partial, or even no role in the business. This is an item that needs to be explored in-depth on a case by case basis and best discussed with your broker rather than here. The thing to understand is this: when calculating SDE you cannot add back the full amount of that family member's wages unless they are absolutely not involved in business operations. You must determine the fair market replacement cost of hiring a competent individual to perform the departing family member's duties. If you were overpaying your spouse for example, you may add back the difference between what you were paying them and the new replacement employee. If you were underpaying your spouse then a negative add back would be in order. The same holds true for business owners who also own the property from which they operate, where they are essentially paying themselves rent. Proper SDE calculation must have the rent expense normalized to the amount that they will charge the new owner/tenant.

Another area of caution: Personal expenses camouflaged as business expenses can backfire. Aren't these "add-backs?" There is more to it than a simple yes, no, or maybe.

Not too long ago, I sat down with the owner of a successful apparel company in Colorado. To give you some context, this company was raking in revenues of well over $7,000,000. Yet, I was taken aback when I saw a whopping $300,000 in vehicle expenses. Upon probing, the owner explained his passion for performance cars and quickly mentioned that his accountant gave him the green light to run these expenses through the business. The logic? These expenses considerably lowered the business's net income (which flowed through to his personal income), leading to significant tax savings.

I took a pause before commenting on this practice. It's not my business to advise or judge how a tax preparer categorizes what goes on the tax return. These may be allowable by the tax code but also may be pressing the envelope. But I did make it clear to the owner that this was not just an eyebrow-raiser for lenders but also a potential red flag for any educated buyer. When he asked why, I explained that buyers might see this as more than just a "tax dodge." They might wonder, if a business owner is willing to push the envelope here, what else might they be doing that's not above board? Remember that strategies for minimizing tax liabilities may be fine several years before selling but they also may have unintended consequences at sale time - even if your tax preparer is willing to include them.

The way you operate your business might not always resonate with potential buyers. Even a whiff of unconventional practices can make buyers doubt other, entirely legitimate aspects of your business. Buyers and their advisory teams weigh the risks far more heavily than the opportunities. Make sure your operations stand up to scrutiny. Ethical considerations can and do influence a buyer's perception, their offer, and the likelihood of a successful transaction.

THE VALUE OF DOCUMENTATION, INTELLECTUAL PROPERTY, AND LEGAL ASSISTANCE

THE WIN-WIN OF DOCUMENTED PROCESSES

A clear playbook provides Bible-like comfort for a buyer. Buyers don't know your operations. If they don't find documented processes, they may see chaos, and therefore risk. And here's the bonus – once you've documented your operational aspects and shared them with every member of your team, it becomes more than just for the buyers. Your team will have clarity and understand exactly how to do the job correctly. Buyers will have the playbook they require, and, in all likelihood, your business will operate more efficiently, producing greater financial performance in the months and years leading up to the sale.

UNPACKING INTELLECTUAL PROPERTY

You might think your enterprise is just another cog in the industrial machine, but it's not. The unique way you provide your services, how you interact with clients, and the ethos of your business sets you apart. If you're always pursuing excellence and improvement, you'll outshine others. Your business will grow, attract loyal customers, and set new performance benchmarks.

Many years ago I founded a transportation service targeting affluent individuals and wrestled with the challenge of differentiating our business from the competition. On the surface, we were just another service provider like many others. But what set us apart wasn't just our fleet of high-end vehicles; it was something more.

A client interaction with a well-known billionaire's family revealed ours. An act as simple as a trip to a pharmacy to fetch over-the-counter medications for his wife turned into an epiphany for me. They were astonished by this seemingly minor gesture of service. What felt natural to me was a revelation to them. It dawned on me that we weren't just in the business of transportation; we were in the business of making our clients more efficient. This wasn't in our original business plan; it was our innate approach that naturally distinguished us. But to be sure, it became a hallmark of our service impressed upon every member of our team.

When you discover your secret sauce don't keep it a secret. Tell your story in your marketing, instill it daily in your staff, and demonstrate it to your customers every day. Most of all, make sure that you tell your broker! Make no mistake, this is all a part of what makes your business attractive to a buyer.

Here's my challenge to you: Step back and be introspective about each aspect of your business. Recognize those seemingly small actions, ethos, or practices that set your business apart. These are your intellectual property - your business's "secret sauce." These ingredients have helped you carve out a niche for yourself and will serve the buyer extremely well. Make no mistake; it is your unique intellectual property and should be shared with the buyer early and often during the sale process.

That client I served? They became one of our most loyal customers and sent a flurry of referrals our way, which over the years amounted to hundreds of thousands of dollars in profit. This wasn't due to just the type of vehicles we offered or our punctuality but because of our culture of going the extra mile each and every day. You must understand why your customers use the service or products that you provide. In our case it was patronizing a transportation service that saved them time and made them more efficient. We were not simply in the transportation business, we were in the customer productivity business.

What truly adds value to your enterprise is what sets you apart from the competition. Identifying, nurturing, and leveraging your intellectual property will make your business attractive to potential buyers. As you go about this journey, ensure that your broker understands the critical importance of your intellectual property so it becomes an integral part of your business's value proposition.

LEGAL CONSIDERATIONS

Before you sell, please schedule a consultation with a competent Business Transaction Attorney. Understanding the legalities, structures, and contracts associated with your business is essential. Some legal work may need to be done before the sale process begins. Your family attorney might be great, but get a second opinion from someone specializing in business transactions. Have them review your contracts and customer agreements. Can they transfer to a new owner? Address this well before going to the market. Bottom line: Legal advice can seem pricey, especially when it is simply to review your business, but it's money well-spent.

The Importance of Collaboration and Communication

I genuinely believe that the cornerstone of a successful sale is strong collaboration, blunt honesty, and communication between the broker and the business owner. Effective communication before, during, and in the moments leading up to the sale will ensure a successful outcome. There is no perfect business, and each tends to have a problem area or two that a buyer will surface during the sale process. Share these with the broker and formulate a thoughtful and credible response for when the buyer brings it up. In many cases, mentioning and addressing it early in the conversation will make it a non-issue. It could become a deal-killer if it comes up late in the process.

Adapting to Unique Challenges

I recall an encounter a few years back with the owner of a sign manufacturing business—one of the oldest businesses in Colorado, boasting over a century of serving the market. Their situation was dire. Their largest customer had decided to skip a year in their purchasing cycle, severely impacting their financial performance. Their expense burden no longer supported by strong revenues threatened to overwhelm them. They felt they were at the end of the road.

Rather than the usual scenario where I was tasked to sell a profitable operation, I had a far more challenging situation. We were essentially selling assets: equipment, inventory, and, most importantly, a customer list—a list of valuable and recurring relationships built over decades. The immediate question was, how do you put a price tag on relationships, especially when there's no guarantee these customers would continue their purchasing habits under new ownership?

Together with the business owner, we devised a method to

quantify the value of each customer relationship. We knew this wasn't a business for the public market but for a competitor. We initiated what we call our *Targeted Outreach Process*. Together we created a list of their competitors and ranked them based on several metrics: customer compatibility, likelihood of maintaining confidentiality during the sale process, the manner of how they did business with their customers, and financial capability. We started with a list of about 40 competitors and narrowed it down to a dozen who fit the bill. Our targeted outreach process is where it got exciting: within a week, we had a strong buyer lined up. Two weeks later, an offer was on the table that pleasantly surprised both the seller and me.

The deal was smooth, with no strings attached and no lender or seller financing. To the business owner it was pure magic. To me, this was a monumental success. Not just because of a successful outcome but because of the collaboration with the business owner. Together we had built a strategy from scratch, executed it, and achieved a favorable outcome. Your intimate knowledge of your business and the market combined with the broker's adherence to a proven process can produce success.

On the other end of the spectrum, a business that is running at peak performance can be sold at a much higher price than one might initially expect. As mentioned previously, I had the privilege of working with the owners of a diesel auto repair business. From the get-go, I could see it was a gem. The state of readiness set this sale apart: the business was prepared, and the owners were informed, organized, and engaged.

They were the perfect clients—always available, always cooperative. We secured a full-price offer for their business and their property. But beyond the numbers, it was an ideal match in terms of ethos and values between the buyer and the seller.

Whether your business is a century-old institution or a modern marvel, clear-eyed assessments, a process-driven game plan, and the power of teamwork with your broker is critical. Success often finds us at the crossroads of readiness and opportunity, where thorough preparation makes the perfect match for a successful outcome.

KEY TAKEAWAYS

- ⇨ Just as you crafted your business carefully, preparing it for sale requires the same attention and consideration. Objective and thorough assessment, a solid strategy, and teamwork between seller and broker are keys to success.

- ⇨ Selling isn't just about numbers; it's an emotional journey. Trust experts, stay calm, and let their guidance lead you through the twists and turns. Above all, keep your eye on the prize.

- ⇨ A thriving business is easier to sell. If your financial documentation needs work, consult a broker and address issues proactively. Above all, until your broker tells you that your business is ready to sell, don't rush to market but instead follow their lead and get your house in order.

- ⇨ The determination of the most probable selling price range is not based on revenue but on Seller Discretionary Earnings (SDE) multiplied by the industry multiple range for comparable historic sales. Determining SDE is a serious and detailed undertaking, the results of which must satisfy and be acceptable to both the buyer and their lender. Do not fool yourself into thinking that every personal expense run through the business will be acceptable to the lender.

⮑ In calculating the most probable selling price range for the largest Main Street businesses the term Adjusted EBITDA tends to be used. It is very similar to SDE with select add backs (adjustments) but excluding owner salary and their associated company-paid payroll taxes.

⮑ Questionable personal expenses of the seller, even when permitted by the tax laws, may result in concerns about other aspects of the business whether valid or not.

⮑ Your unique approach and ethos set you apart. Identify, nurture, and leverage your intellectual property—your secret sauce makes your business attractive to buyers.

⮑ Successful sales are built on strong collaboration and communication between you and your broker. When preparation meets opportunity, remarkable outcomes can emerge.

CHAPTER THREE
MAKING THE MOST OF YOUR BUSINESS SALE WITH THE RIGHT TEAM

A successful exit tends to hinge on two things: the broker's expertise and the adeptness of the advisors supporting you, the business owner. Together, these factors ensure we extract and realize the most from your life's work. During negotiations, the right team can concretely back up and explain every bit of value that your business offers. Often, you'll find that you've been with some of these advisors for years. Others might need to be brought on board or even set aside if their expertise doesn't align with the mission.

KEY MEMBERS OF YOUR ADVISORY TEAM

Here are the people you absolutely want on your side:

- **Business Transaction Attorney:** This isn't just any attorney. It's not the general attorney or the family lawyer you might already have on speed dial. This needs to be a person whose bread and butter is business transactions. Think of it this way: you'd want to see a specialist when facing a specific health issue. The same logic applies here. Going through business transactions without the right attorney is like having brain surgery with a proctologist! Not ideal, right? You need someone at the apex of their game in business transaction law.

- **The Right Accountant or CPA:** Now, let me emphasize the word "right". Not every accountant or CPA is cut from the same cloth. Some might simply record the numbers, resembling bookkeepers more than actual business guides. You deserve more. Ideally your accountant or CPA should have accompanied you on your business journey for several years, offering insights that only they can, given their unique vantage point. Such professionals are not just number crunchers but business visionaries who see things with a broader lens.

  And let's address another misstep: many business owners only interact with their accountants during tax time. That's a missed opportunity. Those professionals that are solely tax preparers may not have the depth of insight crucial for this important undertaking. They are wonderful at what they do, but we want more than just tax preparation when selling a business. We want insight, foresight, and expert guidance. A business-savvy accountant can be an invaluable resource.

- **Wealth or Investment Advisor:** If you do not already have an experienced and qualified advisor who manages your investments, or at least provides you with guidance this is the time to begin a conversation. Now that the time has come to reap the benefits of the investment in your business, you should get expert advice prior to the sale. There are a multitude of options available for deploying your proceeds and these individuals are far more proficient than your CPA, friend, neighbor, or family member. In some cases setting up the strategy *before* the transaction is complete is a necessity.

- **Estate Planner:** These individuals can assist in answering a pivotal question: Is now the right moment to sell your business? Post-sale, will the proceeds, minus all taxes, fund the life you've dreamt of? If you do not have an estate planner I think it's a wise idea to meet with one so that you can develop a plan. If you do have one please bring them into the conversation about selling your business.

- **An Experienced Business Broker**

Remember, even among these experts, there's room for error and misjudgment. Often, lawyers, for instance, view transactions heavily from their legal vantage point, not always blending in the business perspective. And while the law might seem rigid, there are nuances to it. We may need to push back against certain stances, ensuring they align with the business's real-world issues. Just because something is identified as a "risk" doesn't mean it has a high chance of occurring. It's our job to discern between genuine concerns and present but minimal risks that shouldn't jeopardize the sale. Lawyers outline potential risks (as is their job) but rarely tell you what you should do (not their job). It is important that you balance the risk with the potential cost or ramifications to enable you to make a decision that may derail or squash an otherwise great transaction. Just because a lawyer states that something is a risk does not mean that you should not assume the risk. Understand the odds of it occurring and balance the potential harm in your decision to accept or reject that risk.

It's easy to elevate professionals like accountants and attorneys, placing them on a pedestal. But just as in any profession, there are variations in quality. Start thinking about your current team. Are they equipped for this journey? If not, it's time to make some changes. And finally, it's also important that these advisors understand their role and remain in their lane, not overstepping into the role of the broker. The broker is the maestro of the advisory team orchestra.

THE CORE RESPONSIBILITIES OF A BUSINESS BROKER

Every business owner contemplating a sale wonders, "What will my broker do for me?" It goes well beyond putting a "For Sale" sign on your business.

1. **The Business Owner's Guide:** Your broker helps you understand the entire sales process. This isn't just about numbers. It's about emotions, operations, and financial intricacies. Every business sale gets emotional, and trust me, that's normal. We've seen it all before and will guide you through those turbulent times.

2. **The Marketing Package:** Expect to see a sample Marketing document, Confidential Business Review (CBR), or Confidential Information Memorandum (CIM). Great brokers make it a point to dive deeply into understanding your business and shaping a compelling value proposition for potential buyers via the Marketing document and how it is presented to the market.

3. **Financial Analysis:** Brokers don't take numbers at face value. They may work closely with your accountant, pinpointing obstacles and ensuring no landmine remains undetected that could hurt the sale later on.

4. **Marketing and Buyer Outreach:** A robust marketing plan tailored to your business will target potential buyers. They then initiate conversations with buyers and conduct debriefs with the owner to address any underlying questions or concerns that are likely to arise in subsequent buyer-seller meetings.

5. **The Negotiator:** Once an offer is on the table, an experienced broker will review the offer and highlight the most critical aspects to ensure the terms are in your best interest. They will then negotiate the elements on your behalf while also providing insight into the buyer's interests. Negotiating is not a one-way street, and some degree of compromise should be expected.

6. **The Due Diligence Facilitator:** This step is crucial. Almost 50% of all transactions die during due diligence. Organization of documents, establishing a clear process with deadlines, and holding each party accountable for meeting their action steps distinguishes exceptional brokers from the pack. Broker control of the due diligence process is critical to getting to the closing table.

7. **Getting to Closing:** This journey almost ends at the closing table when the funds are wired to your bank account, and this is also when the broker is paid their success fee. However, the period from negotiating the offer through due diligence and to the closing table is really *where the broker earns their fee*. It is not simply working the process with

the buyer and seller, but all of the other people and entities that are a part of the sale process. Attorneys, accountants, lenders, landlords, appraisers, and other advisors create not just one but multiple juggling acts to get to the finish line. It's for this reason that we always impress upon both buyer and seller to keep focused on the goal, maintain a sense of purposeful urgency, and expect that their stress levels will rise up as they approach the closing day. Managing the emotions of each party is one of the many skills which business brokers must be adept and experienced with. During our due diligence kick-off meeting I let the parties know that emotions are likely to arise and ask them to make me, the broker, the one that they express those emotions to. It is our job to be the voice of reason - even when one party or the other is unreasonable.

8. **Training & Transition**: Let's be sure not to forget that after the funds are in your bank account and you've lifted a glass or three of celebratory libations, you'll likely be back in the building the next day to begin the training and transition period. As a part of the transaction agreement, you, the seller, will have committed to providing the new owner with all of the tools, advice, and guidance that they need to operate the business. Depending on the complexity of the business and the competency of the buyer, the transition period may last from two weeks to many more. The industry standard is 30 days of hands-on training followed by a number of weeks of phone and email support. Most sellers are eager to agree to the training period while negotiating the transaction but quickly lose enthusiasm when the transition period begins. The good news is that in most cases,

if you have followed the sale preparation guidelines in this book, the new owner will have the roadmap they need, and your on-site presence will no longer be required after week two. The new owner will have a strong desire to take charge. Be advised that even though the deal is closed, your ownership has ended, and the money is in the bank, you have a contractual legal obligation to provide the training as promised. Funny things can happen under a new owner, and when challenges arise, or worse, finger-pointing begins, you want to be sure you have done your best to train them to take over the reins. In today's litigious society, protecting yourself is critical.

You can think of us, the brokers, as the experienced and cool-headed quarterback of the transaction. Even if you've been through a sale before, we've been through dozens and dozens. We're the conductors overseeing that each part of the orchestra plays in harmony even though many of the musicians play to their own tune. Understanding not only the buyer and seller but all of the other advisors and participants in the transaction and how to ensure that they perform is one of the most critical skills the broker possesses. There is a very good reason that business brokerage is a rather small specialty profession. It comes without the security of a steady paycheck, and fewer than 25% of those who enter the profession last more than two years. Choose your broker wisely.

CHOOSING THE RIGHT BROKER FOR YOU

Selecting the right broker begins with understanding that the business of selling businesses is both complex and process-driven. In

41

addition to normal professional courtesies (punctuality, responsiveness, etc.), you must make time to understand the skill set and experience of the broker who will represent you in what may be the largest and most significant financial transaction of your life.

By nature of the number of businesses within a specific industry and geography at any one point in time, 99% of brokers are generalists rather than industry specialists. I cannot recall when I have not been asked, "Have you sold my type of business?" It's a reasonable question, but it's not really important to a successful outcome, and in some cases, it can hamper a successful sale. Brokers in the top tier of the profession know that making assumptions is a crutch for those who are not willing to dig into every aspect of the business they are representing. You do not want a broker representing you who believes they know everything about your business or industry. You want a broker who is hungry for knowledge about your business and your market. I mention 'process' frequently, including the process the broker goes through in learning about your business. At the end of the day, your business is unique - even if the broker has sold ones in the same industry. Helpful, yes. Important, no. The overall preparation and sale processes are what count above all else.

The best brokers exhaustively make it their business to know your business, but they will never be an expert on your business, nor should they. Their role is to bring the buyer and seller together by creating and articulating the Value Proposition that makes your business the most attractive on the market. You are the expert, and the questions that really matter to a buyer should be answered by you and only you. It is the broker's responsibility to manage all aspects of the sale process effectively, not to speak for you about the intricacies of your business and industry.

Generally speaking, all businesses are fundamentally the same.

They all have sales, revenues, expenses, customers, employees, vendors, suppliers, and a host of other attributes. A broker with a depth of real-world business experience combined with a solid understanding of the interplay and impact of each attribute, as well as one who is serious about their craft are the minimum qualifications you should be looking for. Credentials matter because they demonstrate that the broker embraces the ongoing mastery of their craft. Organization, follow-up, and attention to detail matter not only because the stakes are so high but because without these skills, it will be almost impossible to achieve a successful outcome. Engaging a broker who has been a (successful) business owner is even better as they understand what it is like to stand in your shoes.

Beyond these, the little things are often early indicators of their dedication to their work, professionalism, and how they will orchestrate the sale process to a successful conclusion. Punctuality, how they dress, respect for your staff, manners, listening skills, eye contact, and mastery of the language also count. This is the person who will be representing you and your business in the market. If they do not have pride in themselves and their appearance to others, it will likely be very telling about how you will be represented.

Experience is a significant factor; it's generally a good idea to opt for a broker who has been actively involved in the industry for more than a couple of years. Being part of a reputable association and holding noteworthy credentials are tell-tale signs of their dedication and professionalism.

Honesty and objectivity are invaluable traits in a broker. As a client, you should seek unbiased advice rather than hear your opinions echoed back to you. The ideal dynamic is when the broker provides direction rather than merely following the client's lead. It's natural as an experienced business owner to want to be in charge of the process but this is the time to put yourself in the arms of the broker. Finding a broker who can relate to your journey, especially one who has previously owned a business, can offer a unique perspective. Building a professional relationship is key, especially considering that you will be collaborating with your broker for an extended period, quite likely for over a year. This relationship doesn't necessitate the bond of friendship, but mutual trust and respect are of the utmost importance.

A broker's moral compass should always point in the right direction. Being fiduciaries, brokers have an ethical commitment to prioritize their client's interests above their own personal interests. Because brokers are only paid when a business is sold, and therefore securing a listing is first and foremost for their success, too many brokers push a prospective client to engage when they are not ready, the business is not ready, or make a promise to sell at an unrealistic price. If a broker is pushing you to sign a listing agreement before you are ready, that is a broker you should part ways with. The sale of your business should be on your timeline, never the broker's.

You must seek objectivity, honesty, and integrity. A great broker will respect and embrace your timeframe rather than their own. They will also detail how they arrived at the most probable selling price range so that you understand it. If the gap between what you need the business to sell for does not match what the business is likely to sell for, then you need clarity of thought to make an informed decision to determine if this is the right time to sell. *Businesses very, very rarely sell for more than the most probable selling price range.*

As a matter of practice, when we meet with a prospective client, we never ask what they think their business is worth or what they need the business to sell for. We do not want anything to cloud our complete objectivity. Does this mean that we may have fewer engagements than our industry peers? Absolutely. But it also means that we sell over 90% of the businesses we bring to market at a price agreeable to our clients. We tell business owners what they need to hear, which is often different from what they want to hear. It's honesty and integrity and the only way we know how to do business.

The process of choosing your broker shouldn't be rushed. Given that this relationship is pivotal to the successful sale of your business, you must find someone with a robust and effective process who comprehends the significance and nuance of the deal and cherishes the trust you place in them.

LOCAL MARKET KNOWLEDGE

A broker with local market knowledge is important, but more than facts and figures, they must possess a feet-on-the-ground understanding of the local geography and the interplay of the business environment in that market. A case in point: A business producing $300,000 in SDE in the greater Denver area would be considered an attractive business, but just 90 miles away in the mountain resort towns, that same business is likely to be a tough sale because a new owner may not be able to afford the cost of housing. In addition, the skilled labor needed to perform the business's services is likely to command a higher wage which will figure into a buyer's future growth plans. As the business owner, you will be a wealth of information for your broker, but you may also be so close to your business that your objectivity may be compromised. Remember, your broker will speak with savvy buyers who will look at all aspects of your business, and merely touting how great your business is will diminish their credibility with a buyer. This is why the most successful brokers, those who attain the highest sales price consistently, tend to be seasoned business people first and foremost.

THE POWER OF A STRONG NETWORK

A business broker's network should consist of connections with industry professionals who can bring to bear their expertise to address and correct issues in your business as well as to provide specific knowledge to your personal situation. An effective broker should have a deep enough network to connect you with the right experts to provide clarity and resolution to the issues which may hinder a successful outcome. Exceptional brokers are creative problem solvers who make it their business to bring solutions to the table.

This network should stretch from SBA and commercial lenders to accountants, bookkeepers, tax, marketing, finance, sales, training, and real estate professionals. I always seek to surround myself with professionals at the top of their respective fields to draw on their expertise to address issues that a client's business may have. No one can master everything, but tapping into a knowledgeable network gives you access to the best advice possible, ensuring the most successful outcome.

TEAM COLLABORATION

How about the dynamics between a business broker and other team members? First and foremost, you, the business owner, should introduce your advisor team to the broker you're working with. Encouraging each to work with your broker cannot be over emphasized. Make it clear that they should be responsive to the broker's requests, whether face-to-face meetings, phone calls, or email exchanges. Once the sale process is underway, delays can cause a deal to be derailed and a fatigued buyer to lose interest and exit the process. You must impress upon your advisors the importance and magnitude of the outcome to you and to your family. It's also advisable to tell them specifically that you will compensate them for their time and for making you a priority.

Every professional has their timelines and way of doing things, and while the broker needs to be sensitive to this, you must remember that time kills all deals. As the advisor's client, you have every right to diplomatically insist upon them having a sense of urgency. Don't shy away from the costs you will incur from your advisors. This is when trying to save a few bucks may cost you thousands. That $400 an-hour bill from your CPA? It's an investment. Every dollar you spend in this process has the potential to multiply and return to you at the closing table.

UNDERSTANDING BUSINESS BROKERAGE FEES

The fees associated with the sale of your business by business brokers are fairly simple and consistent. Most brokers will charge an engagement fee ranging from a couple of thousand dollars to as much as $25,000. In our practice, this fee is returned to the client at closing as a credit to the final success fee. Success fees range from 8% to 12%. If the business does not sell during the engagement period, the engagement fee is retained by the broker to offset their expenses. Remember that selling a business is not like selling a home or a commercial property, and it is neither quick nor easy - if it were, there would be tens of thousands of business brokers as there are in

47

real estate. *Unlike residential real estate there is not a buyer for every business.*

Our engagement fee is on the lower end of the spectrum and varies based on how long we expect the process to take and the likely complexity of the overall transaction. This is not solely based on the condition of the business and the market but also on our sense of how reasonable we expect the client to be. Those prospective clients who appear to be reasonable, realistic and enjoyable to work with will incur a lower fee than those who seem likely to thwart a sale at every opportunity. How do we ascertain the likelihood of a difficult seller? Owners who draw lines in the sand about unrealistic prices or terms are a tip off. Remember that at the end of the day the market is going to determine the value of the business as expressed in the sale price. If your plan is to give the broker 'a shot' at selling you business for an unrealistic price I can tell you from experience that it is unlikely to result in a successful conclusion. A broker who concedes to your unrealistic prices or terms expectations is likely focused on securing your listing and should be avoided. How to know if your price is unrealistic? The broker should take you through how they determined the value so that you understand it. You may not agree with the price range but you will understand how it was arrived at.

While interviewing brokers to represent you, if their engagement fee is above $10,000, you should seek an explanation. If it is to defray their marketing costs, please show them the door. Successful brokers are capitalized well enough to invest in the sale process. If not, this is not the broker for you.

You should also be wary of those who charge less than a 10% success fee. Why? Successful brokers only have so much time and can only handle so many clients at one time. Trust me, if they do take on an engagement at a reduced rate, they are likely to work just a little less hard because the lure of the client who is willing to pay them what they are worth is likely to receive the most attention. It's simply human nature. If the broker is willing to readily concede their rate, in essence, how they feed their family, then this is likely how they will negotiate on your behalf. As stated above, the purpose of the engagement fee isn't simply a way to compensate the broker if a sale doesn't materialize. The more significant purpose of an engagement fee is to act as a testament to the seller's genuine commitment to selling the business.

In the premier Main Street Market, which is usually defined by businesses with revenues ranging from one to thirty million, it's advised to avoid brokers who ask for monthly retainers except in very unique circumstances. Such a system can suggest that a broker is more incentivized by these regular payments rather than the actual sale of the business, which is never in the seller's best interest.

In terms of the final payment calculation, the success fee percentage will decrease as the final sale price increases into the million of dollars. In some practices, like ours, we are fond of the Double Lehman method. This approach calculates the commission with a base percentage rate for the first million in sale value and applies a decreasing percentage rate for each million in sale price. There are also variations of the scaled fee structure, the key being to align the interests of both sellers and brokers to secure the absolute highest sale price.

A few more thoughts on broker compensation. While 10% of the sale price sounds like and can be a significant amount, one needs to remember that:

- Less than 20% of all businesses listed for sale actually sell. The broker who touts how many listings they have as a measure of their 'success' may only sell only a few in the span of a year. The absolute gauge of a broker should be how many of their listings sell at or close to the listing price - not how many listings they have. If you want to judge the quality of their engagements for yourself, ask to see the full marketing package of a few listings that *you* choose from their inventory.

- Your broker will be working for many months, and even over a year, on your business sale. Depending on the business and the local market, prospective buyers may appear soon after the business is brought to market, or after many months for reasons well beyond the control of the broker. Sometimes we have to wait until the buyer finds us.

- Take into consideration what you pay your salespeople. Salespeople choose the profession because they are money-motivated, and brokers are the same. This is likely the most significant sale of your life, and now is not the time to try to save on a commission.

THE PROS AND CONS OF GOING SOLO IN THE SALE OF YOUR BUSINESS

In my time, I've not come across too many business owners who ventured into selling on their own. This is consistent with our ideal client target: they understand that the best outcome is achieved by experts in their chosen field, for the same reason their customers or clients trust them. One way or another, they come to understand the unique skill set and experience that makes us successful, and they also understand that during the sale process, they must maintain 100% focus on the performance of their business. This is not the time for anything less than a total focus on your business, as any deterioration in performance can be the death knell of a great outcome. Using a broker will ensure that your time is spent on the business and not on the many aspects of the sale process which will be disruptive at best.

Here's the raw truth: Selling a business isn't easy. If you're new to this, you'll soon discover it requires balancing and managing a multitude of day-to-day activities that are dependent upon others and where follow-up and communication cannot be slowed. This is far more than soliciting an offer and negotiating a deal to make it to the closing table. During such a pivotal time, your business needs you to be fully engaged to maintain consistent performance. Remember also that the time between an executed offer and the closing date can span many months. Both the buyer and their lender will be eyeing your financial performance every month or week up until closing and any deterioration in performance can change the dynamics of the sale, or worse.

So, what happens when a business owner decides to go it alone? Frankly, the outcomes aren't pretty. Most deals fall through. Owners spend significant time, energy, and emotional capital only to come up short. Worse yet, they might undervalue their business or expose themselves to a multitude of unforeseen risks. It's like leaving money on the table and only realizing it when the transaction has been completed. The few who manage to seal a deal often look back regretfully, wondering if they might have struck a better bargain with expert guidance.

On the flip side, those who've unsuccessfully attempted a solo sale quickly appreciate the intricacies involved. This realization often drives them towards seeking a broker's expertise. Even with a broker, a successful sale isn't guaranteed. Business owners are surprised to learn that fewer than 20% of businesses brought to market result in a sale. Why? Because mediocre businesses that lack documentation and preparedness for sale do not attract serious buyers, and if they do, a lender will not participate in the transaction. However, those who engage an experienced broker and enter the process with the required seriousness stand a much higher chance of a successful and lucrative exit.

I outlined the cons so it's only fair that I mention the pros. Going it alone may allow you to avoid paying the broker's fee. However, it is not likely to provide you with the best price and the best terms, and the distraction of the sale process may very well negatively impact the business's operational and financial performance at the worst possible time. There are very few pros when it comes to trying to sell your business yourself.

KEY TAKEAWAYS

- Specialized expertise in your advisory team, whether a business transaction attorney, a CPA, or a business broker, directly influences the success of your business sale.

- Choosing the right broker goes beyond just credentials; strive for mutual trust, respect, and alignment of interests.

- Transparency in fee structures ensures that you and the broker are incentivized toward securing the best possible sale price. Understand the broker's perspective that the engagement fee reflects your commitment to selling and being fully engaged in the process. Unless there is very sound reasoning, avoid monthly retainers which may better suit the broker's financial interests rather than yours.

- Effective collaboration between your broker and other advisory team members is necessary so that each professional plays an invaluable role in achieving the best sale outcome.

- Selling a business on your own poses significant risks. Owners might undervalue (or more often overvalue) their business, face unanticipated complications, disrupt the performance of the business, expose you to post-sale risks, or simply end up without a sale. Leveraging a broker's expertise increases the likelihood of a successful sale.

CHAPTER FOUR
ACCURATELY PRICING YOUR BUSINESS

L et's face it: in 98% of all cases, business owners are most interested in the most likely selling price of their business. After all, they have spent years, decades, and, for some families, multiple generations building a business that has allowed them to realize the American Dream. Their hard work, time spent away from family and friends, and significant ongoing investment (rather than material rewards for themselves) should be unlocked when it is time to sell.

When I decided to sell the first business I built, I was taken aback, or more specifically, shocked, when the broker told me the value I should expect to receive at closing as it was far less than I believed. I objected and said that he did not understand the hours that I had put in and how much money it would take someone to build the business to this level of quality and sustainability. I expected that he would agree, but he pointed out as emphatically as his nature allowed, "The value of the business to a buyer is in no way based on the time, effort, and money you have invested: the value is based almost solely on the financial benefit (cash flow, income) that buyer will receive."

I was dismayed but quickly understood why this made sense. The price a buyer will pay is a function of the financial benefit to the buyer. It's relatively straightforward with a basis in simple math: Will the business produce enough earnings to provide the buyer with an income, a return on their investment (down payment), and enough to service the debt load required to finance the acquisition? If it does not, the business is priced too high. If it produces significant excess cash after the new owner pays themselves and services the debt, the business will support a higher sale price. As I said, simple. This is why I implore business owners and those reading this book to understand this early and often by engaging with a business broker to *secure a baseline valuation in the years preceding their exit.*

Without a doubt, all business owners will benefit from their first valuation. It allows them to place a stake in the ground from which to increase the value of their business not only via financial performance but also by identifying and focusing on the other value drivers that positively impact the final exit price.

You may be wondering about the 2% of business owners who are not concerned about the sale price, and there are likely more than 2%. These are the owners of failing businesses who want to leave the business and their financial obligations behind. They often find that they do not have the energy, savvy, or desire to operate the business, or they may be tied to a personally guaranteed long-term lease where simply assigning the lease obligation to someone else will allow them to exit without losing their shirt. In today's commercial real estate market especially, you will find that landlords rarely will let you out of a lease. Several years ago one of my broker colleagues had a call from a prospective seller who 9 months prior had invested over $600,000 in establishing a retail store selling Virgin Olive Oil products. The business was located in a high-end shopping mall with a 10-year lease with monthly lease payments of $12,000. After only 6 months of operations the couple realized that business ownership, particularly in the retail marketplace, was not for them. Without question they were in a predicament - and one with no good options. The business, like many start-ups, was not yet profitable and the SDE was in negative territory. As you now understand, SDE is the foundation of value determination and negative numbers cannot support a sale price which would make much of a dent in their $600,000 investment. To compound their pain they were also on the hook for the remainder of the lease period guaranteed by them personally: in effect $12,000 per month for the next 9 years - well over $1,000,000. If they were intent on a near-term exit and were not willing to build the business to profitability it was highly likely their investment would be lost. To rub additional salt in the wound they also understood they were responsible for the lease. In this case they were willing to let the business go for *any price* that could get themselves out of the lease obligation.

FUNDAMENTAL CONCEPTS IN BUSINESS VALUATION

Main Street business businesses typically sell at a price based on a multiple of Seller Discretionary Earnings (SDE). These are businesses with a selling price of up to $2,000,000. Businesses selling upwards of $3,000,000 typically are valued based on a multiple of Adjusted EBITDA or EBITDA (Earnings Before Interest, Taxes, Depreciation, and Amortization). Multiples tend to be specific to those realized by like-sized businesses sold within the same industry category (as evidenced by the sale prices reported by SBA lenders over the past 20 years).

Generally speaking, businesses with SDE of less than $200,000 are sold at multiples of 1.5 to 2.00 times (also expressed as 'x') SDE. Once a business consistently produces more than $300,000 in SDE, it begins to sell in the 2.0 to 2.5 multiple range, and once SDE consistently exceeds $500,000, a seller may obtain a multiple of 2.5 to 3.5, or even higher depending on the industry and other qualitative attributes of the business. One should understand that multiple values do not simply move from 2.0x to 3.0x but instead, based on several qualitative factors, move from 2.0x to 2.1x to 2.2x and so on. It is not only the SDE size but the *overall quality* of the business that will determine (and support) the final multiple.

The vast majority of businesses, if not all, with sale prices under $500,000 are sold to third-party financial buyers (those who will be the owner-operator), as well as many up to a sale price of $3,000,000. Once a business has a sale price above $3,000,000, it may attract attention from both strategic and synergistic buyers. The primary driver of value (price) in the Main Street Business Brokerage segment is SDE, which is sometimes also referred to, but sometimes incorrectly, as Adjusted Cash Flow. EBITDA (Earnings Before Interest Taxes Depreciation and Amortization) is a term that is also used to measure the financial performance of a business. EBITDA tends to be used instead of SDE once SDE approaches $1,000,000 and is the norm in both the Mergers & Acquisition (M&A) and Investment Banking markets. At the highest end of the Main Street business sale marketplace we also use the term Adjusted EBITDA defined previously. Moving forward we will use SDE.

We do not determine the listing price range as a function of the value of the assets unless the fair market value of the assets exceeds the value of SDE times the multiple, in which case the liquidation sale value of the assets will be the larger of the two. It is critical for the business owner contemplating a sale to understand that all of the equipment assets that are required to produce both the revenue and resulting income will be included in the sale price rather than in addition to the sale price. Without these equipment assets, the business cannot produce income. For example, the owner of a pizza parlor who recently invested in a $200,000 imported pizza oven will be in for a surprise when he is told that his business, which produces $125,000 in SDE, is worth $250,000. "How can this possibly be? The oven alone is worth $200,000!" Simply because businesses sell for a multiple of SDE, not the value of the assets. *When the value of the assets exceeds the SDE times the multiple range you are most likely looking at a liquidation sale.*

APPROACHES TO ASSESSING BUSINESS VALUE

When discussing business value we are specifically speaking about the most likely selling price range of the business to a third-party owner acquiring 100% ownership (equity) of the business. There are three primary methods business brokers will use to determine the value of your business:

→ **The Asset Method:** The Asset method, also called the Net Asset Value (NAV) method, reviews the assets and liabilities as reported on the company's balance sheet and adjusts each item to its current estimated fair market value. This approach is used primarily for businesses that do not possess intangible value above their adjusted book value.

→ **Market-Based Approach:** The Market-Based approach tends to be the dominant valuation method for the business brokerage industry. It uses SDE or EBITDA as the baseline figure to which a multiple is applied. These multiples are based on historical sale transactions within the same industry for firms of similar SDE or EBITDA performance. To determine the most probable selling price range of your business, a broker will usually use this valuation methodology.

→ **Income-Based Method:** The Income-Based valuation method determines a business's value by turning the anticipated (future) earnings or economic benefits into a present-day dollar figure. At and below the Premier Main Street (selling prices below $5,000,000), this is a very seldom used approach.

IDENTIFYING VALUE DRIVERS

The most significant value driver for a Main Street business is SDE performance over the last three years, with greater weight placed on the most recent 12 month period. Scale does matter, which is why a business producing $600,000 in SDE will have a higher multiple (and listing price) than a business within the same industry producing $200,000 in SDE. As mentioned previously, multiples generally do not move in an entirely linear fashion from a 2x multiple to a 3x multiple (for example). They tend to increase (or decrease) in the multiple range based on qualitative factors such as:

- Consistency of SDE (and overall financial) performance.
- leanliness and consistency of financial data.
- Presence of documented processes & procedures.
- Organizational structure and hierarchy which reduces owner dependency, a General Manager for example.

- Market position, branding, and reputation.
- Barriers to entry.
- The overall appearance of the business and its publicly visible assets - including its public-facing staff.
- Regulatory and/or licensing requirements of the business, owner, or key employee.

As stated previously, a common misconception is that revenue is a significant value driver. *Revenue has little to no impact on the sale price of a business.* Remember, profits are the main driver of the selling price. If the value of a business's assets exceeds the profit (SDE) times the industry multiple (equalling the selling price range), you are probably looking at a liquidation sale of the assets of the business.

THE IMPORTANCE OF REGULAR BUSINESS VALUE REVIEWS

Business owners will be well-served by inviting a broker to provide an Opinion of Value at their earliest opportunity, even if their timeline for an exit is ten years from now, and then have that document updated every two years, a year prior to selling, and finally a month prior to going to market. It's folly not to know the value of your business should circumstances dictate having to sell when you least expect it—more than that, it is an excellent strategic planning tool.

Interestingly, most business owners and anyone with an investment, especially investments for their retirement, check the value of their investments every year, month, or week, and yet they have no concrete understanding of the value of their business. Why would you not want to know the value of what may be your single largest asset - especially when you are in the position to increase that value?

You cannot personally increase the value of your stock portfolio but you can increase the value of your business.

Knowing where you are today will enable you to chart your path and progress towards your destination so that when you arrive, the numbers will allow you to realize the exit you have been working towards for so long. When starting to speak with brokers, tell them upfront that your exit horizon is 2 to 3 years out. The one that suggests that you call them when you are a year out should be removed from any further conversation. The ensuing year(s) will allow you and the other brokers time to build a relationship. This will also enable you to determine which broker demonstrates the competence, guidance, moral compass, and fiduciary responsibility to put *your timeline at the forefront*, ahead of theirs.

A great example of obtaining an accurate business valuation well in advance of an exit is my former client, Richard. For over 30 years, Richard and his wife built a strong ski rental business in one of Colorado's most well-known ski resorts. This was a seasonal business in which 100% of revenues came in from November 15th to April 30th. The business was a model of efficiency and consistent profits, which enabled Richard to build the American Dream. It provided for their financial well-being as well as an envious lifestyle.

Richard contacted me in 2020, wondering what the value of his business was so that he could plan an exit on his terms. In essence, a financial planning equation. When would the after-tax sale proceeds combined with their savings and social security income enable them to retire without compromising their lifestyle? The business was valued between $550,000 and $700,000 at that time. Richard understood that the numbers would take another five years to add up to the reality of an exit and we agreed to remain in touch to chart his progress.

During our subsequent 'check-ins' we took a deep dive into the business from an operational standpoint to ensure that when the time came to sell, the business would command a sale price at the top end of the value range. This included organizational hierarchy, brand, financial and process documentation, and developing a right-hand person who might remain with the business post-sale.

We communicated quarterly over the next two years to ensure he met the "qualitative" aspects that would set his business apart. Not surprisingly, because he initiated many of the value-driving actions we suggested, the business operated more efficiently. Revenues increased as a result, but more importantly, profits increased at a higher rate. When we met for our quarterly check-in and valuation update in late 2022, we determined that the business would now command a sale price between $1,050,000 and $1,200,000. Richard realized that the numbers would now add up, and the exit he had dreamed of may be at hand.

We had a compelling story and brought the business to market in early 2023. Within three weeks, because of the attractiveness of the business, we were fortunate to create a structured auction process and chose the buyer who, in our estimation, was the best to take over the reins and continue on the legacy Richard had built. The business sold for $1,175,000. Was this luck or simply inevitable? Truth be told, it was like many successes, where planning, preparation, and action moved the exit date forward significantly. Be assured that while we suggested what actions he should take, he is the one that delivered. We were only the guide.

KEY TAKEAWAYS

- ⮑ Main Street business sale value is *primarily* determined by SDE, times the multiple range and adjusted upwards or downwards, based on a number of qualitative factors. Adjusted EBITDA and EBITDA are used for Premier Main Street and larger businesses.

- ⮑ Revenue is less significant than profit in determining a business's value with assets playing a lesser role.

- ⮑ The market-based approach, using historical business sale data within the same industry, is the most common valuation method for businesses with selling prices under $5 million.

- ⮑ Consistent SDE, clean financials, established procedures, organizational structure, and a strong market position are key value drivers influencing higher valuation multiples.

- ⮑ Regular valuation updates are important strategically, enabling business owners to plan and potentially increase their business's value in the years before the sale process begins.

- ⮑ Understanding and implementing value drivers helps ensure a business will realize a sale price at the upper end of the value range.

- ⮑ Building relationships with trustworthy brokers well ahead of the intended exit will make it easy to identify who has your best interests in mind, understand your business, the market, and is ultimately the best fit for you.

CHAPTER FIVE
IDENTIFYING AND ENGAGING THE MOST PROBABLE BUYER

Understanding who your potential buyers are is a core element of the sale process. Far too many businesses' daily operations and services revolve entirely around the business owner. In such cases, when the owner leaves, no one is left to deliver the specialized services or the unique value the business is renowned for. Finding not only a financially qualified buyer but one with those same unique talents can be extremely difficult, which is why these businesses can be virtually impossible to sell, and if they are, much of the value will be left on the closing table.

If you've invested your heart and soul into your business, it's hard to imagine it running without you. But here's the reality: Businesses heavily dependent on their owners often face challenges when it's time to sell. On the flip side, those businesses with strong teams, especially those with a reliable second-in-command, are the golden geese. They attract a broad spectrum of buyers, and the larger the pool of buyers, the higher the potential sale price and the quality of the buyer you can expect.

To give you a practical perspective, when I assess a business for sale, one of the first things I begin thinking about is the potential buyer and the size of the buyer pool. Geography plays a crucial role here. If your business is in a remote town with a limited population, it automatically shrinks the pool of buyers because only a few may be willing to relocate to a distant location, especially if it's only to operate a business. Consequently, businesses in such areas often struggle to fetch a price on par with the industry average—simply because there aren't as many buyers vying for them.

Imagine you have a business that multiple parties are interested in; the dynamic changes entirely. Instead of hoping to attract a buyer, multiple buyers are competing for your business. It's like an auction where everyone's trying to outbid each other. Suddenly, the conversation shifts. Potential buyers no longer think, "How can I snag this business at the lowest price?" Instead, they wonder, "What do I have to offer to ensure this business becomes mine?"

The Advantage of a Vast Buyer Pool

Reflecting on a past client and one of my first as a business broker, I vividly recall a successful but small tree surgery business I had the opportunity to represent. This wasn't just your run-of-the-mill tree service; they specialized in intricate tree takedowns and complete tree care. The owner had carved out a comfortable living for himself, with the business generating between $150,000 and $200,000 in annual SDE. However, the largest challenge was that he was the only one in the entire operation who knew how to perform a technical tree takedown, let alone climb 100-foot-tall trees. And at 62, he was eager to pass on the reins. In addition, he did not retain his team year-to-year which meant that he had to rebuild a portion of the team every year. This is an example of both an owner dependent business and one which lacked a tenured complete team.

This was not going to be an easy sale as he lacked the organizational structure which buyers seek. The potential buyer needed both the finances, a very specific skill set, and to be prepared and willing to build out a team from day one. How many individuals possess the financial capability and the technical prowess for such a niche role? The buyer pool was extremely limited. Over a year, despite our concerted efforts, finding a suitable buyer became a task like finding a needle in a haystack, and no buyer was found. This early learning experience cost me a lot of my time, but for that business owner, it cost him the funds he was depending on for his retirement.

On the opposite end of the spectrum, the smoothest and most successful exits I've handled had a common theme – the business had a sizable pool of potential buyers. In these, the new owner doesn't necessarily need to replicate the technical expertise intrinsic to the business. Instead, they should be adept at leadership, process, sound business management, and managing the team that delivers the service.

A former diesel auto repair client had it all - from meticulously crafted procedures to a structured hierarchy complete with a general manager and a shop foreman. The new owner didn't require prior knowledge about diesel auto repairs. Their role was to chart strategy, marketing, finances, and, most importantly, to ensure that the business continued to produce sustainable cash flow. They would be working *on* the business rather than getting their hands dirty working *in* the business. If they decided to take a little time off, the establishment wouldn't miss a beat—the foreman would guide the technicians, and the general manager would oversee the day-to-day.

An analogy: The CEO of a mega-corporation like Procter & Gamble could seamlessly transition to lead a completely different enterprise like American Express. It's not necessarily about industry familiarity but rather management and leadership experience. Many individuals exiting the corporate world will buy a business outside of their prior industry because they have the skillset for managing and growing an organization. These individuals also tend to be the ones to grow their new business to the next level.

Remember that a wide buyer pool is versatile, allowing for various potential successors, each bringing your business a unique flair and vision. The broader the buyer base, the more likely you are to fetch a higher sale price and a successful sale.

CREATING THE PERFECT BUSINESS DESCRIPTION AND TARGET AUDIENCE

Your business needs a compelling description to captivate the right audience. When you decide to let go of something you've painstakingly built, you must ensure it resonates with potential buyers. Take, for instance, selling the diesel auto repair business. An interested buyer isn't just browsing for fun. They're trying to gauge if they have what it takes. A well-crafted description of the business customized to the most probable buyer set is imperative. Once you have a strong value proposition and the target audience identified you can move forward in executing the marketing plan. We cast a wide net, using not only multiple "business for sale" platforms to create wide visibility but we also make it a point to laser-target potential buyers. Think competitors, strategic or synergistic partners, investors, *as well as* financial buyers. Remember the tree surgery business I mentioned earlier? While we listed it across various sale platforms and contacted buyers from our proprietary buyer database, we also focused on competitors in the region. Unfortunately the other elements of the business were not compelling enough for a sale to a competitor. As always, a successful sale is based on the combination of all aspects of the business, not even profits alone.

The key here is balance. While your description needs to paint an attractive picture, it should also be honest, clear, and pragmatic. The aim is to attract *qualified* buyers, not every potential buyer.

So, do brokers sometimes throw the net too far and wide? Absolutely. This is a pitfall I've seen way too often in the industry. Some brokers create broad and generalized descriptions that fail to allow potential buyers to assess their personal fit with the business. Painting a picture that allows buyers to screen themselves out is as important as enabling them to picture themselves as the owner.

The last thing you want is to engage with a buyer who realizes midway through the sale process that they're not cut out for operating the business. Not only is this an exercise in futility for the broker and buyer, but it also distracts you—the seller—from your primary role of running the business during the critical selling process.

ELEMENTS OF A QUALITY PRESENTATION

Your business broker should include the following to make the presentation of your business stand out from the crowd:

- **History and Structure:** Provide a detailed background of the business, outlining the history and organizational hierarchy.

- **Clear Financials:** Understandable and accurate financial statements are paramount. They help paint a realistic picture of where your business has been, where it now stands, and the prospects of where it may go.
- **Comprehensive Description:** Touch upon all aspects - employees, suppliers, market opportunities, and potential growth areas.
- **Competitive Landscape:** A brief overview of your competitors and an honest but objective discussion of how you fare against them.
- **Opportunities for Growth:** A realistic picture of growth opportunities showing the buyer that they can take the business to the next level is imperative to crafting a compelling story.

The quality of your presentation is a reflection of your business's professionalism. A shabby presentation can indirectly label your business as disorganized, hinting at deeper operational issues, not to mention the perceived quality of the broker representing you.

Showcase the business's features, but always highlight its benefits, including financial gains, a desirable lifestyle, or, ideally, both. While incorporating photographs to liven up the presentation is great, remember to avoid misleading depictions. You don't want to glamorize your business so much that it appears too good to be true, drawing in unqualified buyers. Instead, create a document that resonates with the buyer you want to attract. It's a delicate balance of revealing the strengths, addressing the weaknesses, and painting a realistic yet compelling picture of what one can expect. Puffery or outright false depictions will result in agony in the sales process: buyers do not like to be misled.

Transparency

While highlighting your business's strengths, never dismiss its challenges or weaknesses. Your prospective buyer should see the business without any sugarcoating. Surprises during the due diligence process can be deal-breakers. Presenting a business that doesn't truly reflect its reality is not just a waste of everyone's time but also detrimental to the entire sale process. I've witnessed deals falling apart at the last minute because the buyer got spooked by undisclosed challenges or inconsistencies in the business's portrayal. Be sure to disclose to your broker areas of your business which may be of concern to a buyer. The broker should be able to determine the magnitude of the issue and how to best present it, if at all.

And on a candid note, I have a particular approach when it comes to client engagements. I only work with businesses that meet a very high-quality standard. Many business brokers might be less stringent, but remember, just because a business is on the market doesn't mean it's good. This is why less than 20% of businesses listed for sale actually get sold.

All businesses come with risks, and no business is perfect. A potential buyer is interested in your business because of its proven success. However, there's always room for improvement, and the right buyer might have the skill set to turn your business's weak points into strengths.

Communicating Effectively with Potential Buyers

My advice on communicating with buyers is straightforward: with utmost honesty and a sense of urgency. Remember, the aim is to transition your business into hands that genuinely value it and can sustain its legacy.

It baffles me when I hear about brokers getting back to prospective buyers after their third or fourth call. It's not just about professionalism but about ethics and best practices in our industry. Every call, every inquiry, represents a potential sale of your business. As you begin to screen brokers, make note of how quickly they respond to your call or email. If your broker is not attentive to you, you can be assured that they will neglect potential buyers.

Going deeper into the buyer-seller interaction, it becomes apparent that knowing the business isn't enough. The real art lies in understanding the buyer's alignment with the business. A worthy buyer must bring more to the table than deep pockets, management experience, or industry credentials:

- **A Transferable Skill Set:** Their past experiences and skills should be applicable and required to operate the business.
- **Cultural & Team Alignment:** Their personality should resonate with your business's existing culture which will help enable them to lead and guide the team.
- **Financial Preparedness:** Even the most passionate and financially qualified buyers can falter without the financial means to weather the unexpected.
- **Commitment:** Finally, they should display an unwavering seriousness and dedication to the business acquisition process.

There are countless individuals out there who like the idea of owning a business but lack genuine intent. As brokers, we often sift through numerous inquiries to zero in on the real contenders. Many are just dreamers who will never complete the transaction.

To truly embark on the business ownership journey, three elements are essential: a pertinent skill set, sound financial strength, and, perhaps most importantly, courage. Surprisingly, it's often the latter that's missing. Owning a business is no small feat; it requires betting on oneself, taking risks, and leading with conviction. Every business owner, including you, is a testament to the courage common to business ownership.

TIPS FOR BUYER/SELLER MEETINGS

Negotiation often evokes thoughts of clever tactics and power plays in the context of selling a business. But in my experience, the real foundation of effective negotiation is transparency and clarity. An early word of advice: come to the negotiating table understanding that compromise will be needed and knowing your "absolutes." If you cannot budge on one item, conceding on another may serve you well.

When you're communicating with potential buyers, be clear and direct. Your goal should be to give them a transparent view of what the business is, what it offers, and whether they can truly thrive in its environment. Buyers seek both a financial and personal investment in this new chapter in their lives.

Understanding the buyer's motivation, goals, and skill set early in the screening process can mean the difference between a successful sale and a missed opportunity. You'll need to have tough but necessary conversations in some instances. If you feel a potential buyer may not succeed in your business due to specific constraints or challenges, it's better to communicate those concerns openly and allow them to counter your concerns.

For every hesitant buyer, there's one who only needs a little encouragement. Recall your beginnings when you were unfamiliar with every nuance of your industry. By sharing your journey and emphasizing the strength and structure of your business, you can instill confidence in a buyer, ensuring them that they, too, can achieve success.

Each interaction with a potential buyer is a step closer to finalizing the sale. However, for the unprepared, buyer-seller meetings can be minefields, and I've seen many promising deals collapse due to easily avoidable pitfalls within buyer-seller conversations.

Be careful not to unnecessarily amplify inherent and normal business risks or create undue concerns. Don't create smoke where there isn't a fire. To illustrate, consider the common question about the challenges of running a business. Many owners point to employee retention and recruitment when asked about their biggest challenges. But isn't this a universal concern in the grand scheme of business? Instead of presenting it as a significant hurdle, reframe it as a shared challenge that all businesses face. For instance, rather than complaining about the difficulties of finding good help, emphasize the proactive measures your business takes to seek, nurture, and retain talent continually.

DECIPHERING BUYER'S INTENTIONS

When I work with sellers, one of the earliest discussions we have is to understand the requisite qualifications and the intentions of a potential buyer. More succinctly, what skills and experiences will be required of the buyer to operate the business, and what are their expectations for the near and long term? So, what questions should you, the business owner, be asking?

Start with the basics: Why do they want to buy your business?

Are they looking for a passive investment, or do they plan to manage and expand the enterprise actively? What is their vision for the business's future, and how do they plan to finance the purchase? These questions help in gauging the buyer's strategic fit and financial readiness. Your broker will have covered many of these in the vetting process, but hearing the answers directly from the buyer will be beneficial.

Remember, the cultural fit matters. Your business isn't just a set of financial statements; it's a living entity with a team, a culture, and a legacy. If a potential buyer's objectives clash with your business's ethos, they might not be the right fit, regardless of the price they offer.

Price is, of course, a significant part of the deal. But beyond the numbers, think about the team you've nurtured over the years and their future well-being. You'd want the incoming owner's personality and style to resonate with them. This is why personalities play a significant role. A confrontational or caustic buyer could destabilize the very foundations of your business, especially if there's a seller financing component in the transaction, which may put your future sale proceeds at risk.

FOSTERING TRUST

If I were to offer just one piece of advice, it would be to foster unwavering honesty in all conversations. Both sides must be forthright, open, and genuine in their interactions.

The best transactions I've managed involved buyers and sellers who mutually committed to success, fairness, and a willingness to compromise. Compromise is key. Don't be penny-wise and pound-foolish. Negotiations should always involve ironing out the finer details, and both parties should be prepared to consider both large and small concessions to reach the finish line.

But here's a cautionary tale. Trust is fragile. I witnessed a nearly flawless transaction take a lousy turn not long ago. The seller was happy to provide the buyer with an extended training and transition period. The buyer, after months of smooth interactions, abruptly questioned the integrity of the seller just before closing. They brought in a second accountant to review the financials two weeks before closing and told the seller directly that it was to make sure that what they had been told (and already confirmed) was 'true and correct'. While this should have been a minor, last-minute confirmatory review, the language of their email suggested that they were now doubting the seller's word, honesty, and integrity. Had they posed their request for 'another look' in a phone conversation with me, rather than an email to the seller, it would likely have been received far differently. This drastically shifted the dynamics. Post-sale, the once-eager seller became distant and strictly adhered only to what was contractually obligated, depriving the buyer of invaluable insights and support during the transition. Trust, once broken, is challenging to mend.

THE BUYER-SELLER MINDSET

In another past sale the buyer was the epitome of a professional. Experienced and astute, they approached the business with a balanced perspective, recognizing that no venture is without its imperfections. Rather than being daunted by the business's weaknesses, they saw them as challenges to be overcome and opportunities to improve financial performance. They'd say things like, "I can address that," or "I have the resources to improve this." Their proactive and positive attitude was a refreshing change.

What made this buyer truly stand out was their realistic yet optimistic approach. They understood that every business, no matter how well-oiled, may have faltered occasionally. Instead of sweating the small stuff, they focused on the larger picture. Their commitment to sealing the deal without letting trivialities sidetrack them was refreshing. Trust was fostered early and throughout the sale process. I hope that prospective buyers reading this will approach their negotiations similarly.

The most commendable shared trait was both parties' mutual emphasis on a win-win transaction. They genuinely believed in ensuring that both parties left the negotiation table satisfied. They practiced honesty, showcased patience, and emphasized fairness throughout the process.

Contrasting this experience with other, more tumultuous sales has reinforced a lesson for me. The buyer and seller's attitude and approach are pivotal in the transaction's outcome. As you and your broker consider potential buyers for your business, look beyond the surface. Seek buyers committed to mutual success for both themselves and you, the seller. In our practice, we have a simple maxim: both parties win.

KEY TAKEAWAYS

- Identifying likely buyer prospects is crucial for a successful business sale; having a broad pool of potential buyers can lead to higher sale prices and better outcomes.

- A well-crafted business description is essential to attract the right audience and should balance attractiveness with honesty and clarity.

⮑ Transparency about your business's strengths and weaknesses is vital to avoid deal-breaking surprises during due diligence.

⮑ Effective communication with potential buyers should be honest, timely, and aligned with their intentions, skills, and commitment.

⮑ Building trust between buyers and sellers is key to a smooth transition, and both parties should prioritize fairness, compromise, and a win-win mindset throughout the transaction.

CHAPTER SIX
The Importance of Your Business Story

S ad to say, but businesses do not sell themselves. The value and attractiveness of a business lie not only in the financial performance but also in the whole 'story'. This includes the history, the market, milestones, competition, opportunities for growth, and the benefits of ownership. While presenting the facts is imperative, it is the *sizzle that sells*. This is not to say that embellishing is acceptable, but presenting the business in its most favorable but true light is critical. For example, let's say that you have a Janitorial Supply business that you are ready to sell. To you it may be a rather staid and boring business. You have to identify and present to the buyer what makes it an attractive business. If you cannot get excited about your business it will be very difficult to get a buyer excited. Your broker should help you to tell a story that will resonate with the market. However, remember that false claims can create expensive consequences, especially if adverse material facts are undisclosed. Objectively stating the facts, including strengths, weaknesses, challenges, and opportunities, will describe the business accurately and build trust with prospective buyers.

STORIES SELL

Everyone likes a good story, and most Americans love a success story. If you have remained in business for more than a few years, there is good reason for a buyer to expect the business's performance to continue under their ownership. However, this is not the place to allow them to connect the dots: you must specifically outline all aspects of the business so that little can be left to the imagination, with one exception. It is crucial to craft a solid Value Proposition for the business to enable a buyer to imagine themselves at the helm.

This is also where you can eliminate buyers who have no business in the ownership role. Key elements include what led the owner to establish the business, the history, customers or clientele, financial performance, the presence of processes and procedures, key milestones, supplier and vendor relationships, growth opportunities, and challenges. There are no perfect businesses, and yours is no exception. Be honest and accurate above all else. If you portray the business as all roses and no thorns, you will diminish or destroy your credibility, weakening your story.

Business owners would be wise to begin thinking of the positive elements of their business to enlighten the broker as they prepare to craft the business's Value Proposition. As the owner, you are most familiar with your business and why someone should consider the acquisition. I recommend that you ask your customers or clients why they patronize your establishment and read any reviews that may have been posted to understand how your business is perceived. Beyond the accolades and critiques, you will likely discover the unique benefits of doing business with your company. Outside objectivity is especially valuable and will help construct the Value Proposition.

Surprisingly, I have found that many business owners find it challenging to articulate what makes their business stand out from the competition and attractive to a buyer. During our "courting" phase with a business owner, we always ask a simple question: "Why?" The more we know about a business, the better we can communicate its strengths, weaknesses, and areas of opportunity. We review their publicly-facing marketing and advertising and the reviews left by those receiving their services. The court of public opinion provides keen insight from the customer's point of view into what makes the company tick.

In chapter two I mentioned the importance of understanding your Intellectual Property. The unique approach to doing business may be such a matter of course to you that you fail to realize that it is your competitive advantage. It's a story worth telling early and often.

It's All in the Presentation

Experienced business brokers at the top of their game know that how the business is presented to the market is imperative to attract the best buyers and allow dreamers to leave the conversation. Business ownership is not easy, and presenting the business as such is misleading and unscrupulous. In addition to the key areas of focus outlined previously, the prior 3 to 5 years of financial statements should be presented in full with add-back adjustments clearly noted and described as articulately as possible. Some brokers derive the financials from the Profit and Loss statements, while others prefer the Federal tax returns. In the construction of our marketing document we use the tax returns for the 3 to 5 prior years and the Trailing 12 Month Profit and Loss for the current period. This provides greater insight into the most recent and current trajectory of financial performance.

Once we have engaged with a serious buyer, and only then, do we provide the detailed Profit and Loss and Balance Sheets. The reason? Our time, as well as our clients' is especially valuable and we promise them to present only qualified, serious buyers. Many very successful brokers, including the one who brought me into the business, have their own way of presenting the financials. Get to know the broker and ask them how they do it. There is no right or wrong way because a serious and engaged buyer will dig into all the financial statements as they move through our process. As always, accuracy, clarity, and consistency must rule the day.

In my view, brokers who are willing to engage with numerous small and unlikely-to-sell businesses become accustomed to taking shortcuts in creating their marketing materials. This is not only detrimental to their clients but also to themselves and their commitment to honing their craft. Laziness and shortcuts become the norm, negatively impacting their clients' business positioning for a successful outcome. If your broker does not have an innate commitment to quality in all that they do, you can be confident that they will bring that same mediocrity to the process of selling your business. For that reason, I highly recommend that you ask each prospective broker for samples of their marketing materials from an actual client's listing. It only takes a few minutes to redact critical details, and if you have signed a mutual Non-Disclosure Agreement, the broker should not hesitate. If they do, move on.

BALANCING BROAD AND TARGETED APPROACHES TO FINDING BUYERS

Experienced brokers identify the most probable buyer pool early in the engagement process. We begin to formulate our marketing plan outline after our first introductory meeting. We discuss and confirm our thoughts with our clients and probe them to uncover ones we may have overlooked. Once we know who our most probable buyer is likely to be, we determine how to best reach them with our marketing message. Casting a wide net, in addition to a highly targeted approach, helps to ensure that we leave no channel untapped.

Online marketing is a given in today's environment, but reliance on this alone will likely prolong the sale process and not attract the best possible buyer. At the same time, depending on the business's type, size, and quality, there are many occasions where a highly targeted approach is impossible or will not provide as many potential buyers as we would like.

In the best of cases, we attract multiple buyers who will compete for a business through a *Controlled Auction Process*. In today's Main Street business sales arena, there is one dominant online business sale platform and many vertical industry platforms. For our larger engagements we use a number of subscription-based platforms to reach the Private Equity audience. Understanding the appropriate prospective buyer audience and using the correct tools to reach them tends to produce the best results.

CREATIVITY COUNTS

There are a limited number of marketing options available to brokers, and where a buyer will come from is often surprising. The broker must discuss in depth with their client who the most probable buyer is and how best to reach them. Unique and highly specialized businesses may require a significant depth of expertise from the buyer to maintain and grow the business's success. As Willie Sutton, the infamous bank robber, is purported to have said when asked why he robbed banks: "Because that's where the money is," getting to the correct buyer audience is critical to success. A creative broker will spend a considerable amount of time investigating where to find a unique and qualified buyer, and this is where they stand out from the crowd.

A few years ago, we had the opportunity to represent the manufacturer of highly specialized scientific measurement instruments. Due to the unique nature of the business and the very narrow market of readily identifiable potential suitors, our buyer was, by all counts, virtually invisible. Casting a wide net across the "usual" online business sale platforms was unlikely to produce a buyer. In fact, we were likely to be looking for a buyer who was not actively seeking a business. We had to create demand for this business and identify an individual or business that could become a buyer. This required a diligent, lengthy, and focused effort to find a buyer. Simply posting the business on a public or even subscription-based platform would likely not produce the result we were seeking. All businesses are not created equally. Seasoned brokers understand that without creativity and fortitude it is unlikely that they will find a suitable and willing buyer.

PRIDE STILL MATTERS

When preparing your business for sale from a marketing standpoint, consider every publicly-facing aspect of your business, from how your employees dress to the condition and appearance of your building, public areas, and vehicles. Appearances count, and they can be your silent salesperson or an enemy of your own making.

I recall arriving at a client's restaurant 30 minutes before a site visit by a very well-qualified buyer. My clients were experienced owners of a multi-location and highly profitable restaurant that had served the community for many years. The entrance and dining area were cluttered with the debris of the prior evening's service. I made it my business to begin tidying up when they asked what I was doing. "I'm doing what should have been done last night or early this morning." I did not say this disrespectfully, but they got the point.

Given the months of preparation and work we had invested for this final walkthrough, I was surprised, dismayed, and irritated. How could a professional and successful business owner have so little pride at such an important juncture of the sales process? I won't go into detail about the kitchen but will simply state what the buyer said after the visit: "That was the most disgusting kitchen I have ever seen!"

When the seller asked how I thought the visit went, I pulled no punches and told them exactly what the buyer had said. Incredibly, they said, "You didn't tell us that we should clean before the visit." I was beyond shocked and asked, "If you were selling your home, would you leave your underwear on the living room floor?" They got the message, and thankfully, I convinced the buyer that this was due to the hours the owners had worked the previous evening and that it would be easily cleaned. It's worth saying again: *appearances count.*

We were fortunate, and the deal closed. I am not convinced that my client really understood how close we had come to losing the buyer, but I learned a valuable lesson all those years ago: As a broker, leave nothing to chance. We leave nothing to chance, knowing that appearances always count. For the owner reading this book, I hope I have made my point: Appearances always count and leave nothing to chance. Months of time, effort, and expense can go to naught when laziness sneaks into the process. *Pride still matters.*

KEY TAKEAWAYS

- Successful business sales require effective marketing, emphasizing financial performance and the compelling story behind the business.

- Crafting a solid Value Proposition is essential, allowing potential buyers to envision themselves at the helm while ensuring unsuitable buyers are eliminated.

- Honesty and accuracy in presenting the business's strengths, weaknesses, opportunities, and challenges builds trust with prospective buyers.

- Detailed financial statements, presented clearly with add-back adjustments, save time during initial buyer screening.

- Balancing broad and targeted approaches to finding buyers and creativity in locating unique and qualified buyers leads to desirable sales outcomes.

- Make it your business to view your business as an outsider. Appearances count.

- No matter what business you are in, the pride in your business made it what it is today. Demonstrate that *Pride Still Matters*. It will resonate with a buyer.

CHAPTER SEVEN
WIN-WIN NEGOTIATIONS

After months of preparation, marketing, and discussions, your business has attracted attention in the market, leading to several promising interactions with potential buyers. The anticipation builds until you receive the phone call from your broker, "We have an offer!" This moment marks the beginning of the next critical phase in the business sale process – the negotiation and deal-structuring stage.

This phase begins with the buyer submitting a Letter of Intent, expressly stating their requirements for the terms and structure of the sale transaction. The LOI is the general framework for the transaction. It will be significantly expanded in the closing documents, including the Asset Purchase Agreement, Bill of Sale, Non-Compete Agreement, and others, as well as additional associated schedules and exhibits. While the LOI is not a binding agreement in most states, it will become the foundation upon which the entire sale transaction will be built.

The first thing to understand is that although the agreement in and of itself is not binding, there are two elements of the LOI that are: confidentiality and non-solicitation. The parties agree that confidentiality must continue to be maintained by the parties - this means that both the buyer and seller (and their advisors) must not disclose to anyone other than the parties that they have entered into negotiations or that the business is for sale. Non-solicitation means that as soon as the LOI is fully executed, the business is removed from the market, and any communications with other parties must cease immediately. Aside from these two binding elements of the LOI a buyer or seller can cancel the LOI for any reason, including no reason at all.

It is important to outline the high-level details of the transaction, and the parties must understand that overly rigid or loose elements can lead to misunderstanding, misinterpretation, and stress which may create an adversarial relationship between the parties.My recommendation is that you retain legal counsel to review the LOI prior to executing it. Understanding and balancing the importance of each element cannot be overstated.

CORE ELEMENTS OF THE LETTER OF INTENT

➔ **Total Sale Price:** The total financial consideration for the sale of the business.

➔ **Buyer Cash Down Payment or Equity Injection:** The cash amount the buyer will contribute to the purchase.

➔ **Lender Injection Amount:** The cash amount the lender will put into the transaction, excluding additional monies for working capital, lines of credit, or loan costs.

➔ **Seller Financing Amount (if required):** The amount the seller will finance as a part of the transaction.

➔ **Number of Payments over Time Period:** The number of installments to be paid by the buyer and the number of months the note will be paid.

→ **Interest Rate:** The rate of interest the seller note will be subject to.

→ **Calculation of Interest (Simple or Compounded):** The determination of how the interest will accrue on the seller note.

→ **Inventory Amount:** If inventory is included or excluded in the total sale price and the method in which the value will be calculated, normally at the cost value.

→ **Description of Business to be Conveyed:** (including Real Property if applicable).

→ **Working Capital (if applicable):** The amount of cash or accounts receivables to remain in the business at closing to enable the buyer to meet the near-term expenses required to operate the business after closing.

→ **Closing Date:** The target date for the closing to occur.

→ **Confidentiality Statement:** This statement defines the duration of the period during which neither buyer nor seller teams can disclose that the business is for sale.

→ **Exclusivity Period:** The start and end dates of when the business will be withdrawn from the market and during which no conversations can be had with other potential buyers.

→ **Earnest Money Deposit Amount and Escrow Agent:** If appropriate, the good faith cash amount will be held by the escrow agent and applied to the buyer's cash down payment amount.

→ **Due Diligence Term and Start Date**: The duration of the due diligence period and the start date. These tend to range from 14 to 60 days, with the buyer usually requesting a longer period and a shorter period by the seller.

→ **Lease Details (Assignment or New):** A statement outlining if the seller's lease will be assigned to the buyer or if the buyer will need to obtain their own lease.

➜ **Termination Statement:** The date upon which the LOI will terminate if the parties have not executed an Asset Purchase Agreement or Purchase Sale Agreement (Real Property).

➜ **Governing Law:** The state in whose laws the transaction will be subject to.

➜ **Sale Type:** The determination of the type of sale - Asset or Stock sale.

➜ **Expiration Date of LOI:** The date on which the LOI will expire unless fully executed by both buyer and seller.

➜ **Contingencies:** An additional termination trigger for the buyer after the due diligence period for failing to obtain a lease or transaction financing which are acceptable by the buyer.

➜ **Training and Transition Period:** An outline of the period of time, hours per day, and on-site or remote training that the seller will provide to the buyer.

EVALUATING OFFERS

When we receive an LOI we review it in depth to understand each element of the offer so that we can anticipate how our client, the seller, will likely receive it. If the LOI is missing key elements or includes what I know will be deal killers, I will communicate these to the buyer to seek clarification and advise them on the initial pressure points. Savvy buyers should take these to heart and know that the broker is keenly aware of elements which are likely to be problematic to the seller.

Those buyers who are dismissive of our advice often find themselves creating adversity from the start. As fiduciaries of our seller clients, we represent their interests first and foremost, which means that we also need to provide the buyer with our objective advice - which many times is different from what they want to hear. A poorly crafted offer is best rejected early so that deal killers can be avoided and a productive conversation (negotiation) may begin.

Once we review the initial LOI and address any early potential issues with the buyer, and it is agreed that the LOI is ready to be presented, we schedule a time with the seller to walk through the document point by point. Sellers (and buyers) should understand that the first LOI is a starting point. Taking a deep breath and evaluating every point on its own merit is encouraged so that together, we can determine those items we are willing to accept or reject, and those that will need to be negotiated. Keeping the overall objective in sight and seeking a win for both parties is critical. Sellers should take at least 24 hours to let their thoughts and emotions settle after which a serious conversation with their broker should determine how best to proceed. LOIs typically contain an expiration date of 3 to 7 days, so negotiations must commence without a lengthy pause. Maintaining momentum once a buyer is engaged is paramount to a successful outcome. Remember that *time kills all deals.*

Buyers and sellers should expect counter offers as they are a part of the LOI negotiation process. An experienced broker should have developed a working relationship with the buyer and can speak candidly to support their client's counteroffer. Remembering that most buyers really want to complete a transaction will help grease the tracks for productive negotiations. Digging in one's heels, grandstanding, creating unneeded adversarial positions, or allowing ego to enter the negotiations are sure ways to derail what may be the best offer the seller will get. Seeing things from both party's perspectives will help. The broker should also have the guts to explain to their client when an offer or request is fair and warranted. A few years ago I had a seller client say to me "you represent our interests and it seems that you are agreeing with the buyer!" Sellers must understand that they engaged the broker to *represent* them and their interests to produce a successful transaction, not to *agree* with them if the buyer's contention is valid. In this particular case the buyer's point was extremely reasonable and the seller simply did not appreciate the undue risk it would create for the buyer. Brokers who have a depth of business experience should be able to look at risks from both sides and explain to their seller (and the buyer) when one side is being unreasonable. Sometimes it is not the intent of one party attempting to take advantage of the other, but rather the lack of real-world business acumen on the part of the other party.

One not-so-smart technique I have seen is the submission of a blind offer. A blind offer is one from a buyer who has not had at least one in-depth meeting with the seller. These should be rejected. The underlying goal of these "buyers" is to appeal to the seller's emotions with a full or even higher than full-price offer so that the business is taken off the market while the buyer tries to find funding or initiate an extended due diligence period. It's easy for a seller to become fixated on what appears to be a spectacular offer and dismiss some ulterior and painful motives. With the excitement and enticement of a higher (and many times unwarranted) offer the seller may begin to concede items associated with the sale. This "nibbling" by the buyer can erode the seller's negotiating strength as the days tick by. On the day the due diligence period expires, these types of buyers will tell the broker that they want to re-trade (change) the price. I cannot express it strongly enough: *reject blind offers no matter how good they look*. Inexperienced brokers tend to stray from the correct process when a (likely) too-good-to-be-true offer is presented. Great brokers became such because they are driven by, and stick to their process, and do not allow the buyer's process to supersede theirs. Allow the process to work its magic.

NEGOTIATION PRINCIPLES

Both parties must understand their absolute "must haves" and be willing to concede items that may impede their ability to secure the truly important ones. We advise our clients to put themselves in the other party's shoes and determine the item's overall importance in completing a favorable transaction. Both parties should be winners in the transaction, fairness should prevail, and petty items should be removed or conceded - although they can be used as a negotiating ploy for the give and take which accompanies all negotiations. We generally recommend never digging in over inconsequential or meaningless items that may cause distrust or create animosity for one party or the other. View and evaluate the entire offer in the whole rather than dismissing it out of hand based on one or two elements which while they may be not exactly to your liking, may be critical to getting an otherwise good deal done. The cliche that it is not a good negotiation unless both parties are a little disappointed never resonated with me. 'Give and Take' is a part of the negotiation process and you should understand this from the start.

Over the years, we have seen seemingly strong win-win transactions go sideways because one party forgets or dismisses the overarching objective: to sell and buy the business on favorable and fair terms for each party. The business sale process is an emotional undertaking for both buyer and seller. An experienced broker will hand-hold each party in the weeks leading up to the closing while reinforcing that the emotions of each are normal and to be expected. This is one of the most critical times during which the broker's experience will keep everyone on a steady course - especially by sensing what is likely behind odd, and other seemingly meaningless or irritating requests from the buyer. Remember that this may be the buyer's first transaction and because they lack your depth of experience, the items they ask for or about while inconsequential to you are of concern to them.

DUE DILIGENCE

The due diligence period is one during which the buyer is entitled to ask virtually any question and see virtually any document in order to be comfortable with the end result - the business purchase. It is a *confirmatory* process meant to confirm the accuracy of the information which has been presented. On occasion a buyer will ask for sensitive information which should not be released at this stage of the process. We always tell them why so that our refusal makes sense from a purely business standpoint, not to be obstinate. This is an opportunity to continue to build trust with the buyer, which goes a long way toward a smooth transaction. Any perceived evasiveness from the seller will create shadows on the business, likely to result in a failed transaction.

Sellers should enter the due diligence process with a sense of urgency, clarity, openness, and willingness to provide the details and documentation requested by the buyer. Anecdotally, as many as half of all deals terminate during due diligence. Either party can terminate the deal, but in most cases, if the broker has adequately prepared the business for sale and both the seller and buyer are coached to understand the process, success is more likely. The broker must manage unreasonable and unrealistic buyers at all times, especially from the beginning. Customer, supplier, and employee names should only be provided to a buyer during due diligence in exceptionally rare circumstances. Intellectual property, customer and employee details, processes and procedures, passwords, etc., should always be handled with care. The specific details may be released once due diligence is complete and accepted, but key details should only be disclosed upon the closing of the transaction. Your broker should maintain a *secure* Data Room for all documents relating to the transaction. Information can be placed in the Data Room appropriate for each stage of the process which will make updating and accessing information efficient, timely, and with security measures to control who has access and when. We begin to populate our Data Room well before our client engagement agreement is executed. This allows us to have the information we need at every point of the preparation and transaction process and it also provides a repository for the client to add the dozens of documents which will eventually be required to complete the sale. The sale process is stressful enough without the added burden of a mad scramble to add documents.

The due diligence process should consist of clear and objective information sharing with a sense of collaboration. Before starting the process, the broker should explain each step, be the conduit for all communication between the parties, and track the progress of each information and document request and fulfillment. Further, the broker should advise both parties that they may become stressed during the process and that the broker should be the first point of contact when emotions begin to run high. This will help temper emotions with the broker acting as the voice of reason so they can deliver the message without emotion. Issues and concerns should be taken at face value and clearly articulated. Sincere and objective questions deserve an honest and objective answer to the buyer's satisfaction.

Due diligence is invasive. Sellers may wonder what is at the root of a buyer's question and buyers may not like the seller's answer. The broker should orchestrate the process well, as they are responsible for gathering and distributing documents, fulfilling requests, providing answers, and managing the process to completion.

THE COSTS OF SELLING A BUSINESS: WHAT TO EXPECT

The costs of selling a business tend to fall into the following categories:

- **Broker Engagement Fee:** These range from zero to as much as $25,000, and in most cases, this fee is credited back to the client at closing against the success fee. If the business does not sell, the engagement fee is the broker's to keep. If the broker requests an engagement fee greater than $10,000, I recommend asking what this is for. If it is for marketing or some other expense that you believe the broker should incur, you may want to reconsider your choice of broker. A competent broker should invest in their business and success, not ask you to bear the risk.

- **Engagement Retainers:** It's not my place to judge whether these ongoing monthly invoices are permissible, but our firm rarely enters into these types of arrangements. I'll allow the reader to do the math with this simple caution: If the broker will earn a substantial amount of income from an ongoing retainer income stream instead of a fee made upon a successful outcome, then it is likely it is in the best interest of the broker to drag their feet. M&A firms have a different model appropriate to the segment of the market they serve. In most cases, the retainer monies paid during the engagement are credited in whole or in part against the final success fee at closing.

- **Broker Success Fee:** For Main and Premier Main Street businesses, this ranges from between 8% and 12%. If a broker is willing to work for 8% (or less), the odds are high that they are grasping for business. 12% for a business with underlying issues and a higher-than-average unlikelihood of selling may be reasonable. I've yet to meet an experienced and successful broker who will discount their success fee. If they do, remember that if they are willing to cave in on the value of their expertise (and income), that may be a leading indicator of how they will negotiate on your behalf. Trust me, brokers earn every dollar - especially when they make it look easy and minimize the distractions to you during the sale process.

- **Attorneys' Fees:** Besides the brokers' fees, attorneys' fees are the next largest cost to both seller and buyer. Do not underestimate the importance of experienced and competent legal representation; do not rely on anyone other than a *business transaction attorney* to represent you. This is a very specialized segment of the legal profession, affecting not only your transaction's success but your potential exposure post-transaction. This is no place for your family attorney or a general attorney. Depending on the complexity, fees for a simple transaction may be as low as a few thousand dollars or even approach a six-figure bill. Interview two or three transaction attorneys to understand their fee structure and personality. They are an essential part of your team and hesitating to pick up the phone for fear of running up your bill should be secondary to getting the protection they provide.

- **Title, Recording, or Escrow Fees**: Depending on the state where the transaction will be completed and the presence or absence of real property a title or escrow company may participate.

- **Accounting/Financial Advisory Fees:** Sellers are urged to include their accountants or tax advisors in the sale process. Depending on many factors, these costs can range from a few hundred to thousands of dollars.
- **Lender Fees:** No fees associated with the buyer's lender should ever be borne by the seller unless the parties have agreed in advance.
- **Taxes & Transfer Fees:** Depending on your locality there may be a variety of taxes or fees due at or shortly after closing.
- **Other Fees:** Like many things in today's world it's the questions we don't ask that create financial surprises. Ask each professional on your team what costs to expect. Your broker cannot anticipate all potential costs nor those you will incur from each advisor.

The deal-making process requires strategic thinking, emotional intelligence, and a deep understanding of the legal and financial aspects. Every element of the Letter of Intent, from the total sale price to the finer details of confidentiality and exclusivity, plays a role in shaping the outcome of your business sale.

In business transactions, the art of negotiation emerges as a key driver of success, creating a mutually beneficial agreement that respects the interests and goals of both buyer and seller. Trust in your advisors and your instincts as a business owner who knows their business best.

KEY TAKEAWAYS

⊃ The Letter of Intent (LOI) is the starting point in the buyer engagement process, laying the groundwork for the transaction, with confidentiality and non-solicitation as key binding elements.

⊃ Successful negotiation hinges on understanding and balancing the importance of each element in the deal, avoiding rigidity or ambiguity that could lead to misunderstandings or an adversarial relationship between the buyer and seller.

⊃ Know your "must haves" in the negotiation, be willing to compromise on less critical items, and always strive for a win-win outcome that is fair to both buyer and seller.

⊃ The due diligence phase should be approached with transparency and preparedness, as it can often make or break the deal, with an emphasis on protecting sensitive business information.

⊃ Brokers should have the intestinal fortitude to tell their sellers when a buyer presents a bona fide objection or a counter offer to an item within the LOI. Remember that your broker is there to guide you to get the best transaction possible. You are not paying them to agree with you.

⊃ The costs of selling a business vary and include broker fees, legal representation, and other potential fees. It is advisable to discuss the fees which might be associated with your unique transaction.

CHAPTER EIGHT
FINANCING THE BUSINESS PURCHASE

Generally speaking, three main components are involved in purchasing a Main Street business. This chapter will focus on the *full acquisition* of the business, where all of the seller's equity interest will become the buyers. There are certain instances where a portion of the seller's equity will remain in the business, effectively allowing the seller to remain an owner. As recently as 2023, the SBA (Small Business Administration) updated its rules to allow a seller to retain an equity interest, but absolute clarity remains uncertain. For the purposes of this chapter, we will focus on the more traditional components:

- Buyer Equity Injection or Cash Down Payment
- Lender Financing
- Seller Financing

THE EQUITY INJECTION

As highbrow as the term sounds, equity injection simply refers to the cash down payment made by the buyer for the business. In essence, it is the immediate equity interest in the business, with the balance of the equity coming from the lender. In cases where the seller is extending some degree of financing, the seller does not retain any equity. Depending on the lender and financial strength of both the business and the buyer, cash down payments will usually be between 10% and 20% of the purchase price. It is left to the lender to determine the final amount of the cash down payment requirement.

Lender Financing

Before we jump into the lender financing part of the sale transaction, it is important to understand the basics of Small Business Administration (SBA) lending. The SBA was created in 1953 as an independent government agency of the Federal government to promote and protect the interests of small businesses. In 1954 the SBA created a program which guaranteed loans to small businesses and buyers of those businesses to encourage lenders to provide financing. Prior to this program the sale of small and medium-sized businesses was significantly constrained by the lack of assets owned by the business that the lender could collateralize. With few assets to take possession of and dispose of, the risk to lenders was so great that it was virtually impossible for a lender's credit policymakers to participate in a sale transaction. The Small Business Administration (SBA) was created to, among other things, generate liquidity in the market to encourage lenders to participate.

A common misconception is that the SBA lends money. It does not. Think of the SBA as an insurer to the lender. The SBA will insure a portion of the acquisition loan if the buyer (debtor) cannot make the payments, and the loan must be written off. Currently, the SBA will guarantee the loan for between 50% and 75% of the loan amount (The SBA Guarantee). This risk reduction to the lender makes it more attractive for lenders to participate in business sale transactions.

Simply stated, the SBA creates guidelines for lenders to comply with to receive the SBA guarantee. However, each lender has unique (and often rigid) internal credit guidelines. Choosing the right lender is critical to getting the transaction to the closing table. Not only do SBA lenders pick and choose which types of businesses and transactions they will lend to, but the ability to complete the loan depends on the quality of the lender team. This includes the client-facing Business Development Officer, the Credit Committee, the Underwriter, and the Closing Coordinator. Each plays an important role in getting to the closing table. Virtually every bank in the United States can participate in the SBA lending program, but only a select number do it often and well, and are included in the SBA's Preferred Lending Program (PLP).

Before we bring a client's business to market, we reach out to multiple SBA lenders to have the business transaction pre-qualified so that we have strong confidence that the business sale can be completed. Experienced brokers will likely have a short-list of SBA lenders that they know are able to get a transaction across the finish line. Unsophisticated and first-time buyers far too often engage with SBA lenders who promise that a deal will get done only to receive a "no" from the lender 30 or 45 days into the transaction process. Buyers are well-advised to seek the advice of a business broker early in the process and to be referred not only to the SBA lenders who they know will lend to the business and particular industry but also to lenders who have demonstrated the ability to complete the transaction.

SELLER FINANCING

The topic of seller financing is raised early in conversations with our seller clients and virtually all conversations with buyers. Buyers and lenders believe that a seller having "skin in the game" and "confidence in the business" is critical to the sale and provides safety to each. While this may strongly resonate with a buyer, the lender is much more concerned with the risk of their capital, and passing a portion of this risk off to the seller is usually the underlying objective.

In addition, if a buyer does not quite have the cash down payment necessary to make the numbers work, the SBA guidelines allow the buyer to make up the down payment shortfall with a seller financing component. For example, on a million-dollar transaction, the lender may require a 20% down payment by the buyer. If the buyer only has $150,000 (or the lender wants the buyer to retain more of their cash in the bank for a cushion), the 5% shortfall can be made up by the seller providing $50,000 in seller financing. If the numbers are close, this can get a deal done, but what are the risks to the seller, and is their "skin in the game" really material?

We always recommend that our sellers be open to seller financing if absolutely required, but we always seek a full and final cash-out without it. Buyers will need to guarantee the seller note personally, but it remains in second position behind the loan and at least in second position to the mortgage on the buyer's other major asset, their home. As a fiduciary to our seller client, why would we set them up for this risk? We hold the seller financing card in our hand and only reveal it as necessary. Seller financing, and the contractual instrument which outlines the terms of the Seller Note is usually secured with a personal guarantee by the buyer. However, each state has its own laws as to the limits of personal guarantees. The seller's attorney can best describe how and to what degree the Note can be enforced in the event that the buyer defaults on their debt payments.

The idea of "skin in the game" is a fallacy. Once the transaction is complete and the seller has dutifully provided the buyer with the training and transition period, the only person with "skin in the game" is the buyer. As a seller, be open to it only if the lender requires it.

For businesses where a lender will not participate, and there are many, offering seller financing may be the only path to selling the business. This does not mean a business is necessarily bad, but it may have too many areas of softness in the lender's eyes to meet their underwriting criteria. An experienced and objective broker should be able to tell you early in the process if seller financing is likely to come into play.

Another aspect of the transaction may include "earn-outs" or "forgivable seller notes." We will only delve into these here to provide a basic overview. Let's return to the above million-dollar transaction. The seller may want or need to sell today but feels that the business's recent and near future financial performance should support a higher selling price. This is the seller intent on a sale price above what the buyer and their lender will pay at closing. In these somewhat rare occasions, the buyer may agree to the higher sale price, but the terms will dictate that the additional proceeds will only be paid out if and when the business produces the projected financial performance. In these cases, *the earn-out should be tied solely to revenue performance* and *never to net income performance*. A new buyer is likely less tempted to defer revenue growth than to manipulate expenses. A seller should never agree to an earn-out based on net income. SBA guidelines do not presently allow earn-outs but have recently agreed that an earn-out structured as a forgivable seller note, or series of forgivable notes may be acceptable.

KEY TAKEAWAYS

- In purchasing a Main Street business, three main components are typically involved: Buyer Equity Injection or Cash Down Payment, Lender Financing, and Seller Financing.

- Equity injection refers to the buyer's cash down payment, usually between 10% to 20% of the purchase price, which varies based on the lender and the business's and buyer's financial strengths.

- Lender financing, especially through SBA programs, is crucial in business purchases. The SBA acts as an insurer, guaranteeing a portion of the acquisition loan, thereby reducing risk for lenders. Understanding the SBA's guidelines and choosing the right lender is essential for a successful transaction.

- Seller financing is often discussed early in the transaction process. It's seen as a way for the seller to maintain "skin in the game," although the primary objective is often to pass on a portion of the risk to the seller. Sellers are advised to consider seller financing only if absolutely required.

- "Earn-outs" or "forgivable seller notes" may be used in transactions where the business's future performance might justify a higher selling price than what can be paid at closing. Earn-outs should be tied to revenue performance rather than net income. Not all SBA lenders will allow a forgivable seller note as a part of their lending criteria.

- The SBA guidelines for business transaction financing include a multitude of requirements but the ultimate approval of a loan will be the lender's alone and consistent with its internal lending criteria. As such, not every SBA lender will participate in every transaction. Having your broker understand which lenders are likely to finance your business transaction should be done in advance of bringing the business to market. In this way they can help a buyer locate a suitable lender.

CHAPTER NINE
LEGAL AND FINANCIAL INSIGHTS

t is incumbent that the business owner understand the magnitude of the business sale transaction. Not only may it be the most significant financial transaction of their life, but it is also a complex legal transaction to which both parties will be held accountable. Finding yourself on the receiving end of a lawsuit is disruptive and stressful at best; at worst, it can be financially devastating.

Over the years, we have seen judgments in favor of buyers in which sellers are obligated to return not only the sale proceeds but also additional monies awarded for a multitude of damages. How to protect yourself? Complete clarity and disclosure of all information provided to the buyer and the disclosure of adverse material facts. Be aware that while your broker acts in your interests, they are legally and ethically bound to disclose adverse material facts, both explicit and implied. When in doubt, discuss the issue, potential or otherwise, with your broker and the attorney representing you in the sale transaction.

BUYER AND SELLER RESPONSIBILITIES

CONSENT

Business owners must have legal consent from all owners, partial or otherwise, to sell the business. This is a conversation to have with all owners of the business prior to the decision to sell. A competent broker will confirm all ownership interests with the seller, check the state website to confirm entity structure, and have all owners complete a simple consent form. The attorneys and lender will also require a similar document to be signed before closing. If a partial owner is overseas or otherwise unavailable, this can delay the closing.

FINANCING

It goes without saying that the buyer must obtain financing for the purchase, and the approval for financing must be obtained as far in advance of closing as possible. This is why the buyer must maintain pressure on their lender until the financing is approved. Another role of the broker is to ensure that the buyer takes all the required steps in the financing process and that deadlines are met. A buyer who does not demonstrate a sense of purpose and urgency during this phase will likely be a problem as the proposed closing date approaches.

CONFIDENTIALITY

Confidentiality is critical not only in the early stages of communication between the parties but also up to and after closing. Obviously, the employees will be made aware of the change in ownership. Controlled and well-conceived communication with customers and suppliers is especially important to minimize potentially negative impacts to the business.

OPERATIONAL OBLIGATIONS

In transactions that include an earn-out or forgivable/contingent seller note, the buyer may be contractually obligated to operate the business in a particular manner, both financially and operationally, to ensure that these deferred monies are not put at risk. Sellers and their brokers are advised to perform a degree of due diligence on the buyer to determine that the buyer has the expertise to operate the business. Entering into an agreement with a buyer who is financially or experientially unqualified is pure folly. In our world, this is a critical part of the vetting and qualification process performed by the broker.

SELLER FINANCING

Seller financing, in the form of a promissory note, must be taken very seriously. The buyer is not only liable for the payment but should have personally guaranteed the note. Failure to perform as agreed will not only injure the seller but can devastate the financial health and future of the buyer.

REPRESENTATIONS AND WARRANTIES

Buyers typically are not subject to many of the "Reps and Warranties" that sellers are. Essentially, the business owner represents and warrants that the business is as presented; true, accurate, and complete.

These representations and warranties typically last from as little as 6 to 24 months and usually 12 to 18 months. If, during this period, it is found that these are untrue, the seller is likely to bear both legal and financial responsibility for each breach. The amount of liability is specified within the Representations and Warranties section of the Asset Purchase Agreement (APA). Sellers should understand that breaches are serious and can be financially devastating – to the point of the entire sale being rolled back and the seller being compelled to pay back the buyer and the lender.

COVENANTS

Other important obligations of the seller are outlined in the Covenants section of the APA to fully abide by the non-compete agreement, employment agreement, training and transition agreement, and other agreements accompanying the APA.

KEY CONSIDERATIONS FOR THE BUSINESS OWNER

Three other items should be brought to the attention of the business owner in consideration of the sale.

→ **Seller Note Standby:** When a sale transaction includes seller financing, the seller should know that this note is second in line behind the lender's loan (meaning that in the event of a default, the lender must be paid prior to the seller receiving payments on the seller note) and that payments towards the seller note may not begin until the conclusion of the standby period without authorization from the lender.

Until as recently as 2023, the seller note standby periods could be as long as the duration of the SBA loan – as long as ten years! That's an awfully long time to wait for your sale proceeds, especially if interest is not accruing.

An important note: It's human nature for a seller and buyer to discuss beginning the early payment of the note. The buyer knows that the seller wants their money sooner, and the buyer may be inclined to minimize the accruing interest as well as being beholden to another creditor. Early in my career, when I was working to reach an agreement with the broker representing the buyer, our managing broker suggested that the easiest path would be for the parties to have a side agreement outside of the transaction - in which payments would commence three months post-closing. This seemed to be a surefire way to overcome the seller's objection to waiting for their money. When the SBA lender inquired about the final terms of the seller note, we stated that they would enter into a side agreement. The SBA lender flatly said that this was not only in breach of the lender's rules but also that this was a loan made under the guidelines of the federal government, that this was illegal, and she would be obliged to report the parties to the regulators. I recall the conversation clearly and was fortunate to be advised as to the seriousness of this path by the lender. We learned just how little oversight the managing broker was providing and that they were jeopardizing our future as well as theirs. Every broker needs to understand the rules and advise their clients accordingly. This is why we advise business owners to engage only with brokers active in their industry associations who have received the credentials demonstrating their ongoing commitment to education. There is no additional cost to a business owner in selecting a credentialled broker; it simply makes plain sense.

→ **Landlords:** Landlords have little incentive to assign a lease to a new owner. The reason is straightforward: The seller has an established track record of lease payments to the landlord, and the buyer has no history with the landlord. If the seller's lease contains a lease assignment clause, the landlord is legally obligated to assign the lease as long as the buyer has the appropriate financial strength. Many leases also have a personal guarantee from the seller, and in some cases, the seller's personal guarantee may not be released upon assignment. As one can imagine, a seller remaining personally liable for payments by the new owner for the duration of the lease is unpalatable. New leases may be created in the absence of an assignment clause, or an assignment may be granted with the hope that the landlord will give the buyer a new lease or lease extension when the existing lease ends. In many cases, regardless of the existing lease, the buyer and landlord will draft a new lease agreement.

→ **Working Capital:** Working capital is, without question, the most misunderstood and complex topic in the transaction process. There are many ways to determine working capital; getting two competent financial experts to agree on the methodology and amount is virtually impossible. For this reason, I will only provide a topical definition for the reader to grasp the concept and leave the experts involved in your transaction to arrive at an agreeable amount.

Working capital is the difference between the company's current assets and current liabilities. It pays short-term debt, purchases inventory, and pays day-to-day operating expenses. These may include payroll, payroll taxes, utilities, and those expenses required to operate the business.

There are a variety of factors that impact the working capital calculation. Businesses that are seasonal or have fluctuating working capital needs from one period to another must be carefully and accurately calculated. Business sale transactions (Asset Sales) below $2,000,000 in total sale price often do not include working capital provisions. The seller exits the transaction, retaining all cash and accounts receivable, and paying off all liabilities (debt) associated with the sale. Therefore, the buyer must provide working capital from day one to meet near-term financial obligations. These funds may come from the lender as a part of the loan package in the form of a line of credit.

For transactions with a total sale price of more than $2,000,000, a buyer may include a working capital amount to be left in the business at closing. The inclusion and amount of working capital are negotiable, and competent brokers should advise the seller that the potential for working capital to be a part of the transaction is a very real possibility.

DOCUMENTATION

The usual and customary legal documents associated with the business transaction include:

- NDA (Non-Disclosure Agreement)
- IOI (Indication of Interest) is typically associated with transactions over $5,000,000
- LOI (Letter of Intent)
- Asset Purchase Agreement (APA)
- Purchase Sale Agreement (PSA) - if real property is included in the overall transaction
- Bill of Sale
- Assignment and Assumption Agreement (assigning contracts)
- Assignment of Registered Intellectual Property (if applicable)
- Seller Note
- Personal Guarantee
- Security Agreement (if applicable)
- Non-Compete Agreement
- Training & Transition Agreement
- Employment or Consulting Agreement
- Offer Letters to Employees
- Bank Loan Documents
- Purchase Price Allocation Schedule (PPA): used to allocate fair value to a company's assets and liabilities upon the sale's completion. Items within the APA may include Equipment Assets, Inventory, Training and Transition, Leasehold Improvements, Non-Compete Agreements, Employment or Consulting Agreements, Assumed Debt, and Goodwill.

It is important for the broker and business owner to confer with the business owner's tax professional and attorney to propose the Allocation of Purchase Price. The reason is that the post-sale tax implications for both buyer and seller are typically not aligned. This discussion should happen well in advance so there is agreement before closing.

As outlined previously, business sale transactions are complex, with legal obligations impacting the seller, buyer, and lender participating in the transaction. These must be memorialized to protect the parties and meet local, state, and federal laws associated with a change of ownership. The Letter of Intent is the document that outlines the transaction and is not in and of itself the legal instrument binding the parties. The Asset Purchase Agreement (APA) contains many sections, including a complete description of the business being sold, financial consideration, representations and warranties made by the seller, and the seller's liability should representations or warranties be violated. Additional documents, such as the Non-Compete, Consulting Agreements, Purchase Price Allocation, Seller Note, etc., are other documents executed at closing.

TAX TALK

Business brokers are prohibited from dispensing legal and tax advice associated with the sale transaction. Federal, state, and local tax laws are complex and subject to change, and the implications to each party will be unique to the parties. Tax considerations surrounding a transaction include short and long-term capital gains, installment sale taxation (associated with seller financing), depreciation recapture, and the standard income tax associated with other compensation paid to the seller. In addition, sales tax liabilities may be created on the transfer of assets at the time of sale.

I hope you are now beginning to understand the importance of meeting with a business broker well before an exit. A broker who suggests that they can advise you on any tax or legal matter is shooting from the hip at best and should be dismissed. Your tax professional should be included in the conversation to explain that in addition to the total sale price, what is most important is the net post-sale proceeds and any future tax ramifications. By adhering to the guidelines and principles outlined in this chapter, you can minimize risks, avoid common pitfalls, and maximize the benefits of their business sale. Ultimately, this journey, while complex, can lead to a rewarding outcome when navigated with knowledge, caution, and professional guidance.

KEY TAKEAWAYS

- ⮑ Complete transparency and full disclosure to the buyer mitigates the risk of legal repercussions and ensures a fair and transparent transaction.

- ⮑ Acquiring consent from all owners and securing financing well in advance are critical steps in the business sale process, and they demand careful planning and diligent follow-through.

- ⮑ Confidentiality throughout the transaction protects the interests of all parties involved and maintains stability in the business's operations and relationships.

- ⮑ Operational obligations, particularly in deals involving earnouts or seller financing, may require the buyer to adhere strictly to specific operational standards to protect deferred payments and ensure the business's continued success.

- Understanding and preparing for the tax implications and legal documentation in business sales is crucial, as these elements significantly affect the transaction's immediate and long-term financial outcomes. Letting your tax advisor and accountant know that you are planning to sell is imperative. This will provide them the insight and time needed to address specific accounting and tax preparation issues that are best served well before the sale process.
- Brokers should never offer or dispense legal or tax advice nor ever sway you from seeking such professional advice.

CHAPTER TEN
CLOSING DAY

inally, the big day arrives, and a somewhat unfamiliar calm washes over you as you head to the closing table. This is certainly cause for celebration, but you can expect that as celebratory as the day is, it is tempered by a strong sense of relief. In many cases, it comes as a surprise to the seller that the closing was somewhat of a non-event. Getting to the closing table is a stressful rollercoaster. In the days leading up to the close, I do my best to coach our seller clients that the last-minute requests by the buyer, lender, attorneys, and other parties associated with the transaction are normal and to be expected.

Quite honestly, the days and weeks leading to the closing are grueling and stressful, and emotions can reach a breaking point. For the seller, the smell of money, leaving behind their routine, and attaining the goal surfaces emotions that they don't expect. For the buyer, the excitement of reaching their objective along with some underlying trepidation or fear of the unknown are natural human emotions.

TIPS TO MINIMIZE STRESS BEFORE CLOSING

→ First and foremost, the closing date should be viewed as aspirational rather than set in stone. The vast majority of transactions do not close on the date set forth in the Letter of Intent.

→ Remember that many parties are associated with the transaction, each dependent on others.

→ The seller and buyer are the most eager parties, except, of course, the broker. Keep in mind that for the lenders, landlords, and attorneys, your transaction is simply another day at the office and that the day's victorious outcome will never approach the significance it has for you.

→ Keep your eyes on the prize and understand that last-minute hiccups are sadly part and parcel with the sale process, no matter how ridiculous. Will you get irritated or angry? Most likely, yes. Take a breath, complete the task, and know the end is near.

→ If you have engaged with the right broker, you can be assured that they have done everything possible to manage the transaction and manage the lender and attorneys to complete it. If the broker has done their job correctly, virtually everything is now out of their hands, and much like the obstetrician who arrives moments before a birth, they appear for the adulation of a successful outcome.

Remember, too, that even though the funds are now sitting in your bank account, you will be back in the office tomorrow, announcing the sale to your former employees and beginning the training and transition process. An important point: If your sale includes seller financing, you will receive a promissory note at closing. This is a negotiable instrument, and the original should be kept in your safe deposit box along with all of the closing documents. Finally, send a copy of the complete closing documents to your tax preparer, who will need them for tax filing purposes.

Do take a moment to savor the sale. You deserve it, and no one knows that more than you. Congratulations.

CHAPTER ELEVEN
TRANSITIONING LEADERSHIP AND LEGACY

As business owners approach the finish line of selling their enterprise, they often envision the conclusion as a definitive end to their journey. However, the reality is that the closing of a sale is the beginning of a new and critical phase: the post-closing and transition period. The pressures and stress of getting to the closing table may result in a post-close, post-celebration "hangover." The seller is relieved that the deal is done, and the buyer likely feels the excitement of ownership and the weight of what lies ahead. Where do they start? How do they announce the change of ownership to the staff that is now theirs?

Over many years, the seller established a clear and regular cadence of their workday. They prioritized and addressed their daily activities with a familiar, comfortable routine, and probably without much thought. For them, it would simply be another day at the office. For the buyer, this is entirely new territory.

In the days leading up to the closing, most of the focus has been on getting the various documents assembled and submitted to get the deal done. The seller is mentally ready to walk into the sunset to enjoy the freedom and flexibility they envisioned. In all likelihood, very little focus or planning has gone into this critical next phase. The Training and Transition agreement in the closing documents outlines the duration of the training and transition period. Still, it lacks both formality and an organized outline of all that needs to be accomplished in an orderly and logical manner.

Further compounding the challenges ahead are sellers' and buyers' personalities and "work styles." If little to no planning is paid to this phase, both parties will likely become frustrated, and the rapport built during the past months will be diminished. The best way to ensure the smoothest and most effective transition period is with a plan. This plan should include a general outline with timeframes agreed to and documented by the participants.

The first step in this discussion must be to communicate the importance of having a plan and that both parties must work together for the best results. The seller is the veteran expert, and the buyer is the novice newcomer to the party. Each must understand that patience and a sense of purpose will help this process.

TRAINING AND TRANSITION

The transition period typically begins with the change of ownership being announced to the employees. Once completed, the seller will walk the buyer through the business's daily operations, how the product or service is sold to customers, how orders are placed with suppliers, how the accounting and business management system operates, and opening and closing procedures. Much of the education process is incumbent on the new owner to revisit the many operational processes and procedures the business has established for day-to-day operations.

The seller must understand that years or decades of experience and knowledge must be conveyed in a short yet critically important period. The buyer must know they have a short timeframe to complete the training and transition period. Depending on the buyer's experience with the business or industry, the period may last from several weeks to several months. We typically see no cost associated with the period unless the duration is more than 30 calendar days, after which the parties may agree to an hourly, daily, or fixed rate. The initial portion of the period is usually done in person and on-site, after which phone and email support will make up the balance.

As one might expect, the ongoing presence of the prior owner can create some uneasiness or questions about who the staff should be reporting to. I have found that the new owner is ready to take charge after the first week or two, and the seller's time commitment falls off dramatically. It goes without saying that the seller should help the buyer as much as possible for a smooth transition.

Buyers must remember that how they treat the seller during the previous sale process will likely impact them during the transition period. Antagonizing the seller during the process rather than building goodwill will diminish the transition's effectiveness. The seller may limit their activities to only meet the requirements agreed to in the closing documents and no more. Collaboration and building trust between the parties is paramount to a good relationship post-transaction.

Only a few months ago, one of my seller clients called me two days after the closing in a state of frustration and concern. He arrived at the office ready to begin the transition, and the buyer spent the first three hours on the phone speaking with utility providers, the owner's banker, friends, family, and their investment advisor. The buyer should understand that the training and transition period has a firm beginning and ending date and that this time must be used wisely.

TIPS FOR AVOIDING POST-CLOSING CHALLENGES

➔ Sellers should not be expected to actively manage the business while the new owner is in training. The buyer is now fully at the helm of their new ship.

➔ Sellers must not forget or resent the amount of time they committed to for the training period.

➔ Sellers should diplomatically defer to the new owner for decision-making and staff communication.

➔ The seller must understand that even though the transaction has been completed, they are legally bound and responsible for providing the training and transition as outlined in the agreement.

➔ Remember that in the excitement leading up to the sale, each party may cheerfully agree to one arrangement only for the seller to find it a burden later or that the buyer expected more from the seller. As documented in the Training and Transition section of the closing documents, clarity of expectations is critical.

➔ The best way to minimize conflict and maximize the effectiveness of the transition period is to build upon the relationship fostered during the sale process.

➔ A wise broker will remind the parties that they will be working together after the sale is completed and will check in with each party in the following weeks to provide a quiet word to each party if and as needed.

NEW AND UNFAMILIAR ROLES

Sellers will likely face various emotions once they part from the business. Despite their eagerness to move on to the next phase of their lives, they may feel a general sense of loss: loss of power, identity, and control over their daily routine. However, business owners who have been able to sell on their own terms gain a newfound freedom and a great sense of accomplishment - as they should.

By the time the training and transition period ends, the sense of loss is replaced by a real sense of unencumbered freedom. In the months, weeks, and days leading up to the sale, the seller will typically have begun a mental list of all they will do once free from the daily responsibilities of operating the business. What do they do with all of this time on their hands? Virtually all of my clients have told me how quickly they find plenty to occupy their day and embrace the freedom that comes with their exit.

KEY TAKEAWAYS

- ⮎ Effective post-closing transitions require a well-documented plan that considers both the seller's and buyer's responsibilities and expectations, focusing on a smooth and structured handover process.

- ⮎ Training and transition periods should be respected and utilized wisely, with both the seller imparting their knowledge and the buyer actively engaging and taking charge of the new responsibilities.

- ⮎ Post-closing challenges are inevitable but can be significantly reduced through proactive planning, understanding roles, and maintaining a good relationship built during the sale process.

- ⮎ Both seller and buyer must remember the legal and ethical obligations tied to the training and transition agreement, ensuring a commitment to the success of the business and each other's goals.

FINAL THOUGHTS

Remember that the manner in which you are managing your business for the long term is far different than how you must manage your business in the two or three years leading up to the sale. The extent to which you take a critical eye to your preparation during this period will have an impact on the outcome and final sale price. Just as no two businesses are entirely alike, the factors which impact a sale will vary depending on your business. Below I have added a few thoughts not elsewhere mentioned.

Two Businesses Under One Operating Entity

If you have been operating what amounts to two separate businesses but filing a single tax return you need to take action early and *well before* entering the sales process. For example, we recently had a business owner who operated both a sod farm and a commercial landscape supply business with a single Profit and Loss, Balance Sheet, and tax return. While you cannot easily turn back the hands of time to accurately reflect two independent business operations you must address this situation as soon as possible. Here's how:

review the past two or three years' Profit and Loss statements and for each year create a detailed Profit and Loss for each operating unit (business) with income and expenses clearly and fully documented for each. *There must not be any overlap or duplication of income or expense.* The income and expenses of the two Profit and Loss statements must add up to the totals found on the tax return, not closely, *to the dollar.* You must then have your accountant sign-off on each Profit and Loss to attest to the fact that they are true and correct as presented by you. Unless you are reading this on December 31st it is likely that you are currently using a single Profit and Loss for the combined operations. This is the time to begin documenting the income and expenses for each operation on their own Profit and Loss and Balance Sheet and to file a tax return for each entity. This will require establishing a new Tax Identification Number (TIN) for one of the entities. Unless you take these actions, it is highly unlikely that a lender will participate in the sale transaction and also unlikely that a buyer will have full confidence in the accuracy of the business you are presenting. Lenders do not like ambiguity and because the seller rarely has a direct conversation with the buyer's lender the statements must stand alone for interpretation. Clarity for the lender is paramount with little left for interpretation. Be aware that even with these steps, some lenders will be hesitant to finance the transaction, so be sure to have your broker find a lender that will, or seek the advice of an SBA broker who will find a willing lender. We were very fortunate to have the guidance of one of the country's most knowledgeable and experienced SBA brokers. Without them it is unlikely we would have had a successful outcome. Leaving this up solely to the buyer, especially a first-time buyer, is more than likely to delay or kill your sale.

PERSONAL EXPENSES

If you are running personal expenses through the business in order to minimize your tax liability, and your plan is to sell within the next two years, I suggest that you stop doing so. In establishing the range of value as a multiple of SDE, business brokers are permitted to add back those expenses that your tax preparer allows under the current tax laws. However, lenders will dismiss many personal expenses in their decision-making process. Having a clear understanding of the most likely selling price range as well as confidence that the lender will agree with the valuation will help eliminate surprises. The easier you make it for the lender the easier you make it on yourself. Always remember that it is not just the buyer who needs to agree to the valuation, it is the lender that will make the final decision not only based on your documentation but also the results of the third-party Business Appraisal which the lender uses in their final approval. The dollar you may save in taxes today may cost you multiple dollars in sale value at the closing table.

STRATEGIC INVESTMENTS IN THE BUSINESS – WILL YOU REAP THE BENEFIT?

From both a business owner and business broker perspective I highly recommend that you take a hard look at both your expenses as well as any investments you are making in areas for long term growth. I had a client who was intent on building an internal sales team to focus on national account sales. Two years and $175,000 into this initiative it had failed to produce any significant returns and yet they were still throwing money into it. When asked when they expected to see business from this effort they told me it was still a couple of years out. When asked about their exit timeline they said "in the next 12 months"! If your timeline for an exit is less than 3 years from today and you are investing for something that will most likely not pay off until *after you sell* you are not only wasting precious dollars today and in the period leading up to the sale but each of those dollars may equate to 2, 3, or even 5 dollars in sale value (SDE times the Multiple).

LEARNING FROM THE MISTAKES OF OTHERS

The mistakes I have made along the way, especially in the early years of my entrepreneurial journey, are many. At the time they did not seem to be missteps or mistakes; they were unfounded concerns about letting my vulnerabilities show, my ego, or simply ignorance.

- Get to know your competition. I was afraid of cozying up to my competitors for fear of showing my ignorance or giving away my secret sauce. This mistake cost me months of knowledge I could have picked up and applied to my business. It's a funny thing – competitors will tend to share their experiences and expertise. It's good to get to know them while leaving your ego at the door. You will be smarter sooner, able to make sound decisions more quickly, and accelerate the performance of your business.
- Join and participate in your industry association. It's a sure-fire way to build your knowledge and your business.
- Find a mentor within your industry and share your challenges. It's a lot less lonely when you have an ally at your side who has faced and addressed the same issues.

- Hire a coach. I never did for various bad reasons, mostly because I thought I was pretty smart and did not need help. Every professional athlete has a coach, even Tiger Woods. We all have blind spots and need a proverbial kick in the ass once in a while. If the greatest golfer to step on a course values a coach, so should you.

- Join a Peer Advisory Group. While your business may have a degree of uniqueness, all businesses have the same elements: revenues, expenses, profits, customers, suppliers, and employees. Business owners all wrestle with the same issues and decisions. A Peer Advisory Group with its years of collective experience will provide insight, knowledge, and the confidence to address challenges and grow your business.

- Make decisions. Every day, you will make decisions, and when faced with an especially tough or complex decision, many people will put it aside or push it far into the future. *Failing to make a decision is a decision in itself.* Gather the facts, seek counsel, make the best decision possible with the facts at hand, and move forward.

Evaluating Business Brokers

When evaluating brokers, note their questions and whether they genuinely listen to your answers. The details always matter, and the number and depth of the questions from the broker are a telling indicator of how thorough they will be with vetting and educating prospective buyers and how they will manage the sales process.

Generally speaking, while it is nice to like your broker, it is far more important to gauge their experience, skills, and commitment to process. You want them to ask you tough questions and to respectfully challenge your responses - this is how they will vet prospective buyers.

With a significant sale (and yours is!), there's no room for sugar-coated truths or being told what you want to hear. If a broker is buttering you up instead of giving you the straight facts, show them the door. Top-tier brokers will always be straightforward. They're the ones who'll point out if your zipper is undone - metaphorically speaking, of course.

Just as in any industry, there are experienced pros, soon to be pros, and the mediocre. Make the time to meet more than one, and give them your undivided attention when you meet with them. Failing to respect their time is a surefire way to be removed from *their* list of who they will work with.

I've mentioned 'process' repeatedly throughout this book. If you fail to be engaged and serious about the importance of the sale process, a great broker will quickly recognize it, and quite frankly, if you don't show that you care enough to be serious about the sale of your business, why should the broker?

EPILOGUE

You would not be reading this book unless you were a business owner who has already achieved success, if for no other reason than having the courage to reach for the stars and believe in yourself while others sat idly by. Your ambition and perseverance are commendable, and now, these have brought you to the threshold of another significant achievement - understanding the art of selling your business.

You should now have a basic but solid understanding of the business sale process. With the guidance of a successful, experienced, and highly competent business broker, a lucrative exit on your terms will likely be within reach. This knowledge is a transformative power that can reshape your future and the legacy of your business.

However, I must add a note of caution. Few things are sadder than the business owner who worked a lifetime with the goal of living a comfortable retirement and found at the end of that journey that they had accepted the advice they *wanted* to hear rather than the objective advice they *needed* to hear. You absolutely cannot turn back the hands of time when preparing to sell your business, but you can assure a successful outcome if you make the time to learn and embrace the guidance that a business broker specializing in the preparation and sale of businesses offers.

If the information presented in this book resonates and excites you, I urge you to take the following steps:

- **Commitment:** Make a commitment to yourself to engage a business broker to understand the value of your business today and what you need to do to prepare for a sale, regardless of how far into the future that may be.
- **Planning:** Accept that you will eventually exit your business. Make time to understand what drives a successful exit and begin to implement the actions which will support a fruitful exit. These actions will very likely improve the performance of your business along the way. This is really an opportunity to have your cake and eat it too.
- **Seek Authoritative Counsel:** Don't blindly accept advice from those not actively selling businesses daily. You will be confronted with anecdotes and misinformation from far too many sources. Seek authoritative counsel.
- **Choose Wisely:** Choose a broker carefully, and don't be shy about hearing what you would prefer not to hear. Objectivity, competency, experience, honesty, and emotional professionalism are the hallmarks of the broker that you want to work with.

As you embark on these steps, remember that transformation is an ongoing process. A business owner who commits themselves to preparing early for their eventual exit will reap the benefits of a high-performing business with significantly greater profits and enjoy more free time knowing that their business can operate successfully in their absence. Let me say this again: *Preparing your business for sale now will increase your profits in the near term and increase the sale value at exit.* The vast majority of owners assume that the preparation process is costly and complex - it is neither.

For those who wish to discuss the *Lucrative Exit Process* or seek personalized guidance, I am always here to help. Feel free to contact me directly or reach out to one or more business brokers credentialed by the International Business Brokers Association (www.ibba.org). One hallmark of my success has been making the time to help others - a call or email will always be responded to.

Email: gregg@rockymountainba.com
Phone: 303-474-5582
Website: www.rockymountainba.com

Unlock the value of your business and ensure your legacy. Explore our *Lucrative Exit Process* with a no-obligation, confidential Discovery Call. Let's discuss your goals and prepare a tailored strategy together. Secure your future - book your conversation today.

Email gregg@rockymountainba.com
or call 303-474-5582

ABOUT GREGG KUNZ, CBI, M&AMI

Gregg Kunz has been an entrepreneur at heart since he was young. He founded multiple businesses in his teens, showing early signs of business savvy.

He graduated from the University of Arizona with a BA in Business and Languages. He started his career in New York, quickly climbing from sales to senior executive management roles with global responsibilities after being recognized for his leadership skills, performance, and strategic business insight.

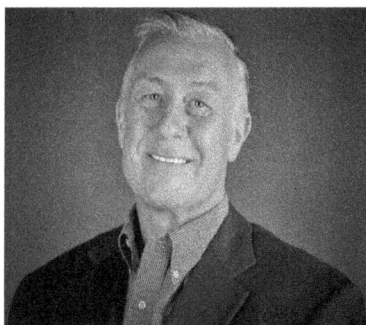

Driven by a commitment to customer experience excellence, Gregg transitioned from the corporate world to entrepreneurship. He went on to start and grow several companies, each leading to highly lucrative exits. Since entering the business brokerage industry, he has been recognized for sustained exceptional performance and is a multi-credentialed industry expert.

Gregg is passionate about sharing his wealth of experience and the hard-learned business lessons. His goal is to guide business owners toward celebrating the rewards of a successful exit designed on their terms. He selects clients serious about a successful exit, often working with them years before the final sale.

A strong supporter of small business owners, Gregg believes these individuals are key players in the American success story, having the courage to step out of their comfort zone and distinguish themselves in a world where many are hesitant to take that leap. His commitment extends beyond business; in his rare free time, he loves skiing, exploring offbeat travel destinations, and mentoring business owners who want to leave a lasting impact.

WHAT GREGG'S CLIENTS ARE SAYING...

"I found Gregg through advertising in a magazine and felt like he was putting himself out there much better than any other brokers. He marketed himself well, which made me hopeful he could market us, the business. I had a brief experience with another broker who undervalued my business significantly. Gregg, however, valued and sold our business for much more, literally getting us a lot more money than we thought.

Before listing, we had several considerations, like being an S Corp for taxation reasons and applying for a green card. Since Gregg sold 95% of all businesses he listed, it inspired confidence that he would help throughout the transaction. I greatly appreciated that he was always there to step in with the right answers and handle the technical aspects.

Gregg did everything he said he would do without overstating or overselling. He was very factual and supportive and kept the whole process going smoothly. Having him in the middle to ask the hard questions and keep everyone on track was invaluable, especially when personal interactions could have potentially gone badly. It's a huge value to anyone thinking about selling a business."

- Richard M., Owner, Snow Sports Equipment Rental Business

~

"Before working with Gregg, my biggest challenge was not having any information on how the process works. It made me feel nervous and anxious. But it was a night and day difference after starting to work with him. I felt at ease and comfortable knowing that Gregg knew what he was doing.

The results were more than what I expected. We got the full asking price and acceptable terms without jumping through too many hoops. Gregg looked out for pitfalls on our behalf, and the results couldn't have been better. To any business owners thinking about an exit, I would tell them to rely on Gregg's guidance and expertise more than anything."

- John J., Partner, Specialty Automotive Repair Business

~

"Deciding to move forward with a broker was a two-year journey, contemplating and pulling the trigger. I was in a mentorship and exit strategy group for 11 years, so I kind of knew what was expected at a C+ level. The real uncertainty was once I decided to go down this road, wondering what kind of can of worms I'd open up, especially concerning when to inform my ops manager, office manager, and employees about the future of the business.

After working with Gregg, the process went a lot smoother than

I thought. Having all my ducks in a row with financials and everything needed made it streamlined. We found the ideal candidate for the purchase and knew we had the right person. The biggest focus was keeping the legacy going, and we found the right buyer for that. It was kind of like a marriage between the two companies. The new owner came in with raises, 401k, full health insurance, and more for the team. Everyone benefited from the sale, and how much everyone would gain was unexpected. The end result was a plus for all parties involved."

- Brian M., President, Technical Metalworking & Fabrication Business

◦∾◦

"Before meeting Gregg, I struggled with choosing who to trust with such a significant decision that would change our family's life. Our business was our sole support and financial income. But it blew me away when Gregg met me for lunch and brought the data and his knowledge of my industry. His ability to quickly earn my trust made it easy for me not to look back and instead say, 'Okay, let's do this.'

His stability and calmness throughout the process made emotion a non-issue. I built my company over 20 years, starting with me and a pickup truck. I'm usually the emotional one between my wife and I, but his data and experience helped me stay focused. He walked us through the process, and his confidence and knowledge kept all my emotions in check. We've stayed in touch even after the sale, which speaks volumes.

Post-sale, the best feeling is knowing that the buyer and I have a great relationship. We're still involved, and I'm aiding in the transition, transferring all the data. The contract Gregg set up and the terms he arranged gave me full confidence in the outcome. Emotionally, I sleep better at night, knowing I had his guidance and oversight.

Gregg matched us with a great buyer. I've enjoyed mentoring them, becoming more of a mentor than I anticipated. Gregg ensured that the business's legacy continues in the right hands. It's been a fun transition, enjoyable, and exactly what we planned it to be. So thank you, Gregg, for looking out for what's best for the business and all parties involved."

- Tim W., Owner, Asphalt Paving Contractor

~

APPENDIX

The following are the lists of commonly requested documents associated with both the sale preparation process and the sale process for both the seller and buyer. The actual documents required will vary depending on the complexity of the transaction, the parties to the transaction, lender requirements, and requests of advisors associated with the overall transaction process. Preparation and organization of documents will help to ensure the smoothest transaction process for both the seller and buyer.

Preliminary Seller Documents for the Broker

- Prior 5 years of Federal Tax Returns
- Prior 3 Years Profit & Loss (P&L) Statements
- Trailing 12 Month P&L Through the Most Recent Period
- Prior Year Balance Sheet
- Current Balance Sheet
- Copy of Lease with All Amendments
- Complete Equipment/Assets List with Current Fair Market Values

- Determination of Leasehold Improvements – ideally documented.
- Report of Top 25 Customers (Names Masked) with Prior Year Revenue Contribution
- Report of Top 5 Vendors/Suppliers with Prior Year Payment Amount
- End of Prior Year Payroll Summary Report with Owner's Wages & Taxes
- Most Recent Payroll Report Including Owner's Wages & Taxes
- Most Recent Real Estate Appraisal – if Real Property To Be Offered for Sale.

Preliminary Data Room Documents for Due Diligence- Preliminary

- Prior 5 Years Federal Tax Returns
- Prior 5 Years State Tax Returns
- Prior 5 Years Profit & Loss Statements in Excel Format
- Prior 12 Months Profit & Loss Statements (Cash & Accrual Basis) in Excel Format
- Prior 5 Years Year-End Balance Sheets
- Tax Returns from Real Estate Holding Entity (if applicable)
- Documents Related to Real Property
- Current Insurance Policies (Complete)
- Workers Comp Audit (Most Recent)
- PPP Loan Forgiveness Documents
- Complete Equipment List with Name, Description, and Fair Market Values (FMV)
- Equipment Assets Valued at Greater than $5,000 Should Include Brand, Model, Serial Number & FMV

- Maintenance & Service Schedules/Logs
- Vehicle List with Brand, Model, VIN, Mileage, & FMV
- Licenses & Permits
- Leases (Property & Equipment)
- Prior Year's 12 Monthly Bank Statements
- Year-to-Date Monthly Bank Statements
- Customer By Revenue Report – Names Masked
- Vendor/Supplier by Total Payment Amount – Names Masked
- Accounts Receivables Aging Report – Names Masked
- Accounts Payable Aging Report – Names Masked
- Employee Handbook
- Employee Roster with Titles, Roles, Compensation, and Tenure – Names Masked
- Security System Details - Without Access Codes
- Images of Business, Products, and Related as Appropriate
- Organization Chart – Departments & Titles Reporting Structure
- Marketing, Advertising, & Collateral Materials
- Trademark or Intellectual Property Documents

Buyer Documents for the Lender for Prequalification

- Personal Financial Statement
- Proof of Funds – Cash Down Payment
- Bank Statements
- Investment Account Reports – Both Buyer & Spouse
- Copy of Life Insurance Policy(ices)
- A Resume Highlighting Experience and Transferable Skills

Buyer Documents for the Lender -
After LOI Execution & Ongoing

- Letter of Intent
- Confidential Business Review/Confidential Information Memorandum
- Business Tax Returns (Prior 3 Years)
- Business Income Statements (Prior 3 Years)
- Copy of Lease & Amendments if Being Assigned
- Name & Contact Details of Legal Counsel
- Draft of New Lease if Applicable
- Asset Purchase Agreement – Draft When Available
- Filed Articles of Incorporation/Formation
- Operating Agreement Executed by All Members
- IRS SS-4 Form Establishing EIN/TIN
- DBA/Trade Name Filing if Operating Under Any Other DBA/Trade Names
- Title Insurance Company Name & Contact Details – if Real Property Being Sold
- Commercial Insurance Company Agent Name & Contact Details

GLOSSARY

Acceleration Clause

A clause used in a note and/or security agreement which gives the lender the right to demand payment in full if a certain event occurs such as default or if the ownership of the business changes without the lender's consent; sometimes referred to as a "due on sale" clause.

Accounts Payable

The amount of money owed to vendors or others by the Company reflected on the Current Financials of the Company or arising in the Ordinary Course of Business of the Company as of a stated date. Often this information is presented in the form of an "aged accounts payables report" which includes the number of days since the Company was invoiced.

Accounts Receivable

The amount of money owed by customers to the Company reflected on the Current Financials of the Company or arising in the Ordinary Course of Business of the Company as of a stated date. Often this information is presented in the form of an "aged accounts receivable report" which includes the number of days since the customer was invoiced.

Addendum

A written instrument referenced in a legal document that adds additional terms or defines additional detail to a written contract. For example an excluded assets addendum would list assets not included in the transaction.

Agency Listing

Also known as an "Exclusive Agency Listing" or "Exclusive Listing." A written instrument giving the agent or broker the right to sell the assets or stock of a business for a specified time and receive a commission regardless of the source of the buyer.

Amendment

A written instrument that modifies a previously agreed to term or condition after a definitive agreement has been executed. This is different than an addendum because it is not by and part of the original agreement and modifies same.

Amortization

Amortization is the expression of the allocation of interest payment vs. principal payment in a total payment. It is a non-cash expense.

Asking Price/Listing Price

The amount the seller of a business is asking a buyer to pay for the assets or stock of a business which may or may not include specific assets such as inventory, personal effects, receivables and cash on hand.

Assets

Also referred to as "Tangible Assets." Those assets which are material or physical (e.g. inventory, equipment, tools, vehicles, real estate, leasehold improvements).

Asset Sale

This term has multiple definitions dependent upon on its usage:

The means by which a business owner transfers ownership of tangible and intangible assets to another owner without transferring the ownership structure or stock.

The sale of a business enterprise at a price based solely upon the value of the tangible assets - typically when the business is no longer operating or operating at a loss. (Liquidation Sale)

A sale of a business in which the buyer acquires only specific assets (and possibly assumes some liabilities). Unlike a stock sale, the buyer obtains the assets usually free and clear of any liabilities, liens or encumbrances of the seller. The buyer is also permitted to "step-up" in basis on the assets purchased based on their allocated fair market values for tax depreciation purposes.

Balance Sheet

A statement of the assets, liabilities, and capital of a business or other organization at a specific point in time, detailing the balance of income and expenditure over the preceding period.

Basket

The dollar amount set forth as the minimum loss that must be suffered by the buyer before the buyer can recover damages under the indemnification provisions. Deductible Basket: Seller is only responsible for damages exceeding the basket amount (e.g., under a deductible basket of $100, if a claim of $150 is made then the seller must pay $50). Dollar-One Basket (Tipping Basket): Seller is responsible for all damages once damages reach the threshold basket amount (e.g., under a dollar-one basket of $100, if a claim of $150 is made then the seller must pay $150).

Bill of Sale

A Written Agreement By Which One Person Assigns Or Transfers His Or Her Rights To Or Interest In Goods And Personal Property To Another.

Blue-Sky

An expression sometimes used to label the intangible assets (e.g. goodwill) in the purchase of a business enterprise. That portion of a requested price that cannot be supported through the application of established valuation methodology, and which generates in and of itself, no economic benefit.

Breach

means, as to any representation, warranty, covenant, obligation, or other provision of this Agreement or another Transaction Document, the occurrence of any material inaccuracy in, material breach of, or material failure to comply with, such representation, warranty, covenant, obligation, or other provision. To the extent this Agreement or another Transaction Document provides for notice and/or the Right to cure the breach of or failure to comply with a covenant or obligation of a Party herein or therein, such breach will not constitute a "Breach" for purposes of this Agreement until such notice has been given and the period to cure has lapsed.

Business Broker

A Business Broker is an intermediary dedicated to serving clients and customers who desire to sell or acquire main street businesses. A business broker is committed to providing professional services in a knowledgeable, ethical and timely fashion. Typically, a Business Broker provides information and business advice to sellers and buyers, maintains communications between the parties and coordinates the negotiations and closing processes to complete desired transactions. The most qualified Business Brokers hold the Certified Business Intermediary (CBI) credential which is managed by the International Business Brokers Association.

C-Corporation

A normal corporation for federal income tax purposes. The entity itself pays income taxes. Note that when we sell a business, the net proceeds are taxed at the "C" level, then any distributions to the shareholder(s) pay capital gains taxes on their personal level.

CBI – Certified Business Intermediary Credential

The Certified Business Intermediary ® (CBI) is a prestigious designation exclusive to the IBBA® that identifies an experienced and dedicated business broker. It is awarded to intermediaries who have proven professional excellence through verified education as well as exemplary commitment to our industry.

CBR – Confidential Business Review

Confidential Business Review. A document describing the financial and operational aspects of a business being marketed for sale explicitly including confidential information not available to individuals who have not completed a non-disclosure agreement (NDA). Also referred to as a CIM or Confidential Information Memorandum.

CIM – Confidential Information Memorandum

Confidential Information Memorandum. A document describing the financial and operational aspects of a business being marketed for sale explicitly including confidential information not available to individuals who have not completed a non-disclosure agreement (NDA). Also referred to as a CBR or Confidential Business Review.

Closing Documents

The legal documents that are part of a business sale transaction and are executed at the closing table after which ownership transfers to the buyer. Closing documents may include: a definitive purchase contract, promissory notes, mortgage, security agreements, financing statements, subordination agreements, bill of sale, covenant-not-to-compete, consulting agreements, employment agreements, leases, assignments, escrow agreement, releases, tax clearances, director and shareholder consents, legal opinions, environmental opinions, fairness opinions, and IRS Form 8594 Asset Acquisition Statement.

Closing Statement

A statement which contains the financial settlements between the buyer and seller and the cost each must pay. They may be on one statement, or the buyer and seller may each receive separate statements.

Co-Broker – Co-Brokering

Is when a Business Broker agrees to share a portion of the commission with another business broker. Many business brokerage firms and brokers do not co-broker, however several states require co-brokering. For other states it is a decision left to the brokerage or broker.

Corporation

An entity created by or under the authority of the laws of a state, composed of individuals united under a common name, and which for certain legal purposes is considered a natural person. Characteristics of a corporation include: (a) continuity of life, (b) centralization of management, (c) limited liability, and (d) free transferability of interest.

Covenants

Affirmative covenants obligate the seller or the buyer to take certain actions prior to the closing. Negative covenants restrict the seller from taking certain actions prior to the closing without the buyer's prior consent. Negative covenants protect the buyer from the seller taking actions prior to the closing that change the business that the buyer expects to buy at the closing.

Discretionary Earnings or Seller Discretionary Earnings (SDE) or Owner Benefit

- The earnings of a business enterprise prior to the following items:
- Income taxes
- Non-operating income and expenses
- Nonrecurring income and expenses
- Depreciation and amortization
- Interest expense or income
- A single owner's total compensation for those services which could be provided by a sole owner/manager. It is the amount of money a business is able to generate for its owner(s) that can be spent on non-business expenses without any adverse effect on the business.

- Acceptable personal expenses of the owner paid by the business as an expense reflected on the Profit and Loss statement.

Earn Out

An agreement in the sale of a business where the buyer agrees to pay the seller consideration in the future (typically cash) based upon certain future events or performance of the business post-close. Because earn-out payments are contingent on the future performance of the acquired company, they are not included in the purchase price.

Earnest Money

A sum of money given to bind an agreement or an offer. It is usually refundable, but might be non-refundable or partially refundable. Refundable earnest money is referred to as soft and non-refundable earnest money is referred to as hard.

EBITDA (Earnings Before Interest, Taxes, Depreciation, and Amortization)

This is a better measurement of a company's financial performance than metrics like revenues, earnings, or net income, and best reflects the true operating profitability of a business. It removes non-operating decisions made by management such as interest expense, depreciation, amortization, and taxes. EBITDA can be used to compare one business to another and tends to be used for business transactions above the Main Street segment where Seller Discretionary Earnings (SDE) is commonplace.

Environmental Report – Phase I – Phase II

"Phase I Environmental Site Assessments" as referred to in the ASTM Standards on Environmental Site Assessments for Commercial Real

Estate, E 1527-05 (and, if necessary, "Phase II Environmental Site Assessments"), prepared by an independent environmental auditor approved by Lender and delivered to Lender in connection with the Loan and any amendments or supplements thereto delivered to Lender, and shall also include any other environmental reports delivered to Lender pursuant to this Agreement and the Environmental Indemnity.

Equipment

All equipment, machinery, vehicles, tools, and other assets owned, leased, or subject to a contract of purchase and sale or lease commitment, that are used or held for use in the business by the company. See FF&E.

Escrow

A deed, a bond, money or other piece of property delivered to a third person to be delivered by him/her to the grantee only upon the fulfillment of a condition. A portion of the consideration that is deposited with a neutral third party (in the case of an escrow) or withheld by the buyer (in the case of a holdback) to be applied toward future indemnification claims by the buyer. After a specified period of time, any consideration remaining in the escrow or holdback account is released to the seller.

Escrow Period

The length of time after the closing date that the escrow is held before being released to the seller or refunded to the buyer.

FF&E – Furniture, Fixtures and Equipment

FF&E or Furniture, Fixtures and Equipment is a list of a company's assets included in the transaction denoted with the current fair market value of the assets in as-is, where-is condition meaning that the value is appropriate for a buyer intending to use the assets in the same way and location as the seller. It is not book value, depreciated value, replacement cost or disposal value.

Fiduciary
Acting in a relationship or position of trust on another's behalf, usually regarding financial matters or transactions. Fiduciaries must place the interests of their client before their own.

GAAP
Generally accepted accounting principles of the Accounting Principles Board of the American Institute of Certified Public Accountants and the Financial Accounting Standards Board.

Hold Back
From a practical perspective a hold back is the same as an escrow except that it is not held by a fiduciary, but by the Buyer.

IBBA
An abbreviation for International Business Brokers Association. When it comes time to sell or buy a business, choose to work with an experienced IBBA Member who will guide you through every step of the process. Look for the Certified Business Intermediary® (CBI) designation to identify individuals who have met the highest standards for education, ethics and professionalism. The IBBA's website can be found at www.ibba.org.

Indemnification
When one party to an agreement agrees to make the other party financially whole for damages and/or losses for specific risk factors they incur as a result of the transaction.

Indication Of Interest (IOI) or Letter Of Intent (LOI)

A non-binding written legal agreement that outlines the major terms and conditions of a transaction to ensure that the Buyer and Seller are in agreement before expending time and funds on drafting of a definitive agreement. IOIs are typically presented in lower middle market and middle market transactions before an LOI. LOIs are typically used in Main Street transactions.

Intangible Asset

That which has no physical existence but represents value, such as goodwill, going concern value, business trade name, reputation. (See Blue-Sky)

Lease

A written legal document in which possession of a property is given by the owner (lessor) to a second party (lessee) for a specified time and for a specified rent, and setting forth the conditions upon which the lessee may use and/or occupy the property.

Leasehold Improvements

Any article or fixture that is attached to land or buildings. Leasehold improvements paid for by the tenant enure to the landlord once attached to the building. Some exceptions might be telephone equipment and computer equipment.

Lessee

A tenant in an individual or legal entity that has a right to occupy a premise by virtue of a lease with a landlord. (see Landlord)

Lessor

A landlord; one who grants a right to the Lessee to occupy the premises by virtue of a lease. (See Landlord)

Letter Of Intent

A description of the key points in a potential acquisition of a business, drafted to provide general agreement on key issues before proceeding further in negotiations, and is generally designed not to be legally binding on either party.

Limited Partnership

A partnership composed of two or more partners whose contributions and liabilities are limited. A limited partnership requires at least one general partner and one limited partner. The general partner(s) are responsible for the management and liability for its debts. A limited partner has no right in management and his/her liability is limited to the amount of investment.

M&A Advisor

An M&A Advisor is an intermediary dedicated to serving clients and customers who desire to sell or acquire businesses in the lower middle and middle markets. An M&A Advisor is committed to providing professional services in a knowledgeable, ethical and timely fashion. Typically, a M&A Advisor provides information and business advice to sellers and buyers, maintains communications between the parties and coordinates the negotiations and closing processes to complete desired transactions.

M&AMI – Merger And Acquisition Master Intermediary Credential

The Merger & Acquisition Master Intermediary (M&AMI) certification is an elite designation that affords professional growth and marketability unlike any other in the M&A profession. This title distinguishes its holders as seasoned intermediary professionals who have a solid educational background, proven accomplishments in completing deals and a strong passion for the M&A Source and M&A work.

Material Adverse Effect

A material adverse effect upon the validity, performance, or enforceability of any of the terms of this Agreement or any other Transaction Document, or (b) an event or circumstance that alone, or when taken together with other events or circumstances, could reasonably be expected to result in a loss to the Business, would have, or might reasonably be expected to have, a material adverse effect on the Business Assets or the Business, or that would constitute a criminal violation of Law.

Merger

Any combination that forms one company from two or more previously existing companies.

Net-Net-Net Lease (NNN or Triple Net Lease)

A lease in which the tenant (lessee) pays a pro-rata share of normal property expenses such as real estate taxes, insurance, maintenance, etc., thereby assuring the landlord (Lessor) of a fixed income.

Offset (set-off)

A deduction by one against a claim of another; e.g. unknown claims against the assets purchased by a buyer may be "offset" against the obligation the buyer owes to the seller (seller financing).

Option

A written agreement granting to a party the exclusive right, during a stated period of time, to buy or obtain control of property or assets on specified terms, but without any obligation of such party actually to exercise such option.

Owner's Salary - Officer's Compensation

The salary or wages paid to the owner, including related payroll burden.

P&L – Profit and Loss Statement

A profit and loss statement is a financial statement that summarizes the revenues (income) and costs (expenses) incurred during a specified period.

Partnership

A business relationship between two or more persons who join together to contribute to the capital and/or operations of an enterprise, and share the profits and losses (also, see Limited Partnership). Partnerships must lack two or more of the four corporate characteristics (see Corporations) to be taxed as such.

Post Closing Working Capital Adjustment

In a sale transaction, a working capital adjustment typically represents a predetermined amount of working capital the selling company must have on the books as of the closing date. If the actual amount is more than the predetermined target amount, the purchase price is increased by the excess. If it is less, the purchase price is decreased.

Proration

The division of money obligations according to a formulaic calculation. In a business closing, a seller may have pre-paid certain expenses which are assumed by the Buyer. The costs of these benefits are "prorated" between the Seller and the Buyer as part of the closing statement (e.g. prepaid rent, prepaid advertising, security deposits).

Purchase Agreement

The agreement setting out the terms for the purchase of a business. A purchase agreement is the "road map" followed by the buyer and the seller in a business transaction. It would include items such as a description of what is being purchased, the down payment and repayment terms, buyer and seller representations, warranties, and indemnifications, and so on. Also commonly referred to as Asset Purchase Agreement, Stock Purchase Agreement or Definitive Purchase Agreement.

Representations And Warranties

Specific assurances made by Buyers and Seller in a purchase and sale agreement stating that certain statements are true and correct. The purchase and sale agreement also includes specific remedies should assurances made turn out to be false or inaccurate.

Rollover Equity

The amount of equity retained by the selling shareholder(s) is measured as a percentage of total equity of the new company and the dollar value of equity retained. Rollover equity is commonly used to bridge the perceived gap in enterprise value by providing a 'second bite of the apple' in the future when presumably the business is worth more providing the seller with a larger multiple than at the time of initial sale.

S-Corporation

A small business corporation which is treated differently than a C-Corporation for income tax purposes. Normally, it can be used by a corporation with 75 or fewer domestic shareholders when the corporation has only one class of stock. Individuals, another S Corporation, estates, certain trusts, certain financial institutions and tax-exempt organizations may own shares in an S Corporation. An S Corporation may own 100% of a C Corporation. If all the statutory requirements are met, the shareholders can elect to have most of the corporation's income and deductions flow through to the shareholders in a manner like the taxation of a partnership.

Seller Note

A note payable or loan to the shareholder(s) or owner(s) of a business provided in the sale or transition of a company by the buyer. Seller financing is typically used to bridge a valuation gap either where other forms of financing are not available or where a buyer desires to preserve the borrowing ability of the selling company for secured financing. Seller financing is typically secured by a personal guarantee and UCC filings on the assets being transferred and subordinated below all other debt such as bank loans.

Simple Interest

The interest on principal (the outstanding amount borrowed) only as compared to compound interest, which is interest on both principal and accumulated interest outstanding.

Sole Proprietorship

A business owned by one person or married persons. The owner is personally liable for the debts of the business. The business is not incorporated in any form as a legal entity of its own.

Stock Sale

The buyer is purchasing all or a portion of the stock of a corporation and the buyer assumes essentially all assets and liabilities of the seller. In a stock transaction the buyer is generally not entitled to a step up in basis on the underlying assets in the corporation.

This may have an adverse impact on the buyer and buyer is potentially at risk of known and unknown liabilities of the acquired company pre-sale.

Subordination

The act of making an encumbrance secondary or junior to another lien.

Survival Period

The length of time after the closing or effective date during which the representations and warranties must be true and the seller is responsible for indemnifying the buyer (e.g., claims by the buyer must be made on or before that date).

Total Transaction Value (TTV)

The total of all consideration passed at any time between the Buyer and Seller for an ownership interest in a business enterprise and may include, but not be limited to, all remuneration for tangible and intangible assets such as furniture, equipment, supplies, inventory, working capital, non-competition agreements, employment and/ or consultation agreements, licenses, customer lists, franchise fees, assumed liabilities, stock options, stock or stock redemptions, real estate, leases, royalties, earn-outs and future considerations.

Transaction Documents

Refers to this Agreement, the Assignment, the Promissory Note, the Security Agreement, the FIRPTA Certificate, the Employment Agreement, the Pre-Closing Assignment and Assumption Agreement, and all other instruments, certificates, agreements, and documents executed and delivered in connection with the Transaction.

Uniform Commercial Code (UCC)

State laws which regulate the transfer of personal property. Article Nine of the U.C.C. creates a security interest in real property used in business transactions to collateralize a bank note and/or seller financing.

Useful Life

The length of time an asset can be utilized before it needs to be replaced.

Warrant Or Warranty

To legally assure or a legal or binding promise usually referenced with "Representation" as in "Representations and Warranties."

www.ingramcontent.com/pod-product-compliance
Lightning Source LLC
Chambersburg PA
CBHW070928210326
41520CB00021B/6840